UNDERDOG
THE INSIDE STORY OF
HUDDERSFIELD TOWN

AND THEIR
2016-17 PROMOTION CAMPAIGN

RAJ BAINS

Foreword by DEAN HOYLE

GREAT N ORTHERN

Great Northern Books Limited
PO Box 1380, Bradford, BD5 5FB

www.greatnorthernbooks.co.uk

Every effort has been made to acknowledge correctly and contact the copyright holders of material in this book. Great Northern Books Limited apologises for any unintentional errors or omissions, which should be notified to the publisher.

ISBN: 978-1-912101-56-6

Design and layout: David Burrill

Cover images: John Early

CIP Data
A catalogue for this book is available from the British Library

Ma,

Your boy done good x

Underdog

[uhn-der-dawg, -dog]

noun

1. a person who is expected to lose in a contest or conflict

2. a victim of social or political injustice:

   The underdogs were beginning to organise their protests.

CONTENTS

FOREWORD

BY **DEAN HOYLE**,

OWNER AND CHAIRMAN,

HUDDERSFIELD TOWN

When I took over as custodian of Huddersfield Town, all I wanted to do was make a difference and put smiles back on people's faces. The club wasn't in the greatest place in that time and, little by little, I wanted to help get us back closer to the sort of position a club like this should be in. That said, however, last season was far beyond even my wildest dreams. It wasn't until around Christmas that I allowed myself to even consider promotion as a possibility, but from then on, I twigged that this was likely going to be our one and only chance.

Most people probably know the basics of the story and can point to how and why the club turned around on and off the field in the fashion we have, but nobody has ever really represented the mood, atmosphere and growing belief of what it was like behind-the-scenes here, although snippets have come out here and there. I sincerely hope this book will help fill in those blanks, and help you understand how special this story is for our club and fans, because it's unique to us, and couldn't have happened anywhere else.

While it's only right and correct that David and the players are given the praise they deserve, there are people who work within this club that are essential to our success, and we couldn't operate in the manner we do without them. Some of them have been here far longer than I have, and have seen the club change in a more dramatic fashion than they'd ever have anticipated, so I think it's important we highlight those folk too, because there's no doubt in my mind that we wouldn't be where we are without those people, too. This club is a family, it always has been, and always will be - it's only right that we share our good times as much as we have the bad.

In truth, I really don't think what we've achieved will ever be repeated - not exactly, anyway. For a club of our size to pull off what we did on such a small budget in such a short space of time, given what football is becoming as a sport, is in this day and age nothing short of a miracle, and it will forever make me proud to be in some way associated with that. For much of last season, I was as much a fan as I was Chairman, and it's not really since the days of Mick Buxton that I've enjoyed seeing Town play in the way I did then.

Whatever happens to this club in the immediate future - the next twenty, thirty, forty, fifty years - we will always have the experience and memory of last season, and the fondness for the club that comes with it. The fans that were here to witness it, much like myself, will look back on those days full of joy and pride, and that's an integral part of the success, for me. If that is our legacy, then that is more than good enough. After all, we're talking about the width of a goal post, here. Had that penalty gone the other side, we wouldn't be talking about any of this. Football is a game of fine margins - it's important we keep sight of that.

To fans of this club, thank you for your support - it will never be taken for granted, no matter the level of success or failure we experience. Not while I'm at the club, anyway. For those of you reading this from outside of our club and town, I hope you can take away from our story that by doing things differently, and by going your own way, anything is possible. There's no point in trying to repeat what we've done here, because you can't, and it's not as easy as that. At this club we like to lead, not follow - if you want to learn anything from Huddersfield Town, it should be that.

Really, there is no magic in this story - I've always said that those who work hard get lucky. And we've been working incredibly hard.

PROLOGUE:

THE NORTH REMEMBERS

To understand Huddersfield Town the football club, you must understand Huddersfield the town. It's a place that wears its history proudly, outwardly, for all to see. The largest landmark in the area, Castle Hill, was once the site of an Iron Age hill fort, and is today the home of Victoria Tower, which overlooks the metropolitan area below. From the untouched Victorian architecture across the town centre to the remains of a Roman fort, what most assume to be a fairly inconsequential area is far from it.

Having been a hub of the woollen textile industry, for example, business was put under threat by the start of the industrial revolution and sudden growth of factories housing specialist machinery. Sparking civil unrest, the fightback became of such size that army platoons were stationed in the town, and despite their ultimate failure to overthrow the advancements in technology, their actions did provoke Parliament to increase welfare provision for those out of work, and introduce regulations to improve working conditions in the mills.

This attitude and desire to punch above one's weight is a constant throughout the history of the town, and remains to the present day. The birthplace of not only former Prime Minister Harold Wilson, but somewhere Herbert Asquith also spent a portion of his formative years, there is something about this town that gives people the desire to make more of themselves. Not only in politics, either, but in the arts, also - Huddersfield is the only place to have provided a captain of the Starship Enterprise, a Queen of Westeros and the first ever female Doctor Who, with Sir Patrick Stewart, Lena Headey and Jodie Whittaker having all publicly stated how proud they are of where they come from.

Set apart and stood alone equidistant between Manchester and Leeds, it would be incredibly easy for a town of such size to lack its own identity and way of life - but that, fortunately, has never been the case. Compared to areas of a similar size across the country, there's no doubt that Huddersfield has been able to force itself into relevance in the face of overwhelming opposition, in both micro and macro fashions. There is a blatant disregard for bending to the will of the establishment that runs through the vein of the town, and that's no better seen than in the birth of the area's other sport: rugby league.

When workers who were missing pay in order to play rugby union asked if they could be compensated for their time, the powers that be at Twickenham told them that those who can't afford to play shouldn't, prompting what would become the creation of a second code of rugby. Naturally, the vast majority of those affected by the elitist attitude to sport - for those who had the money, union was seen as but a folly, and would not be made a professional sport until 1995, around a full century after league - were from the working class north, using the schism to create their own game. The meeting that made the split formal took place at the George Hotel, in Huddersfield - rugby league continues to be the most popular form of the sport in the north.

It would have been not only easier, but perhaps even more practical, for those involved in making the split happen to just roll over and have their bellies tickled. Rather than take the easy route and admit defeat in the face of overwhelming odds, however, they kicked the hornets' nests and took what came at them head on. That's the same defiance and grit that's at the heart of every achievement made by somebody from this town – we are a people who don't know when they're beaten, or when it's best to stay down. Work is hard and expectations are low, but that has never dampened ambition or spirits. It's an outlook that, inadvertently, David Wagner would one day come to define as having 'no limits'.

But what does any of this have to do with football?

It's simple, really – throughout the history of the football club, its fortunes have closely followed the fortunes of the town, and vice versa. Not the type of team who're awash with supporters or attention from those outside the area given what surrounds them, the town and the team are inextricably linked. To know one is to know both – there are far too many parallels to ignore or pretend the reality is any different. Founded in 1908, the club had reached its first Wembley final by 1920, having only come into existence 12 years earlier. Two years later, they'd go on to lift the FA Cup for the first and only time in their history, before dominating the rest of domestic football for the 1920s.

During that time, of course, is when the area was flush with cash, at the heart of the industrial revolution, and riding high on the wave of being a mill town. It wasn't without complications though, naturally. Having had some early financial troubles, there was an attempt in 1919 to merge the club with Leeds City, who would become 'United' in later years. West Yorkshire rivals, this was fought by a grassroots movement who helped the club raise the money it needed to remain in Huddersfield, giving the team the platform it needed to enjoy the success it went on to - in another town, it's likely that club would've been engulfed by its city neighbour. Not for the first time, it's a signal of this town's instincts to go out on its own.

Consecutive league titles arrived in 1924, 1925, and 1926, giving birth to the thrice champions, making Huddersfield the first club ever to achieve the feat. To this day, only Arsenal, Liverpool and Manchester United have matched it, and Huddersfield retain three stars above their crest in recognition of their decorated history.

Then came the Second World War, and hard times arrived with it. As resources dried up, families lost entire generations and the country had to repair itself, places like Huddersfield struggled. Their industries were hit hard, and they were forced to find new ways of prospering, leaving the town in limbo, having to find new purpose and direction. Similarly, the football club entered its own period of soul-searching. Slowly, as money returned faster to big cities than it did to provincial towns, those clubs became the institutions we recognise today, while former giants like Huddersfield were left to exist in the lower divisions, flitting in and out of financial crisis, losing what had originally made them great.

Although they did somewhat fade into obscurity, becoming one of what was in truth many former champion sides who were left to scrap away from the glamour of the top flight, they did retain some relevancy through association. Arsenal, a club who needed to controversially relocate before finding any success, did so through Herbert Chapman, who left Huddersfield for the London club in 1925, leading that club to the first honours in their history. Similarly, after three years in charge of the club, one Bill Shankly left West Yorkshire for Liverpool in 1959, going on to become their longest serving manager and an immortal of the club, laying the foundation for the most successful period in their history.

Those are, to remove any doubt, two of the most influential figures in the history of domestic football in this country - both of whom cut their teeth at Huddersfield Town before going on to help build two of the biggest and most successful clubs in the game. You can forgive Huddersfield fans at the time who were probably of the opinion that it might never happen for their club again, having had once-in-a-lifetime talent pass through their fingers not once, but twice.

On the field, too, Town were the club who first brought Denis Law down from Scotland, and the team to whom he retains he owes "everything". Signed while he was still only fourteen or fifteen, and made a regular starter by the time he was sixteen, an early offer of £10,000 came in from Matt Busby at Manchester United, which was promptly turned down. Having played under Bill Shankly in Huddersfield, the idea was that Law would go to Merseyside with his manager in 1959, but Liverpool claimed to be unable to afford the player at the time, so a year later he joined Manchester City in a then British record transfer for £55,000 under the nose of Busby, who had again made an effort to secure his signing. Rather than reinvest that money in the team, Huddersfield decided instead to pay for new floodlighting, making it considerably easier on the eye to watch them struggle.

In the years between, big figures in football have come and gone through Huddersfield, and it's been a side that's been far from starved of individual talent, both on and off the field. Frank Worthington, of Halifax, began his long career at Town, before becoming an England international after Leicester City came into sign him after six years of service. Known for playing without shin pads, allowing his socks to gather around his ankles, he's the type of talent that Huddersfield fans long enough in the tooth to have seen him play still speak about with a certain reverence now. Prior to Worthington, there was Ray Wilson, who remains the club's most capped England international. Signed by Shankly fresh out of the army, he spent twelve years in West Yorkshire before moving to Everton in 1964, and would become a World Cup winner within two seasons of making the switch. Still living in the area, Wilson returned to Huddersfield after his playing days and built his own undertaking business, and the club recognised their former player by dedicating their 2016-2017 third kit to his World Cup winning achievement, with some proceeds going to Alzheimer's charities.

Although the club has enjoyed talents such as George Brown, who remains their record scorer with 159 and a central figure during their title-winning years, and Billy Smith, who turned out a record 574 times for the Terriers and scored 126 goals during a similar period of time, neither holds the same reverence Andy Booth does, who remains one of the club's only real legends of the modern era.

Having played 452 times and scored 150 goals across two stints for his hometown club, Booth spent five years at Sheffield Wednesday and had a short loan move to Tottenham Hotspur between his two Town spells. During his first run in the side, his goals helped get Huddersfield promoted from the old division two, and on his return, the Terriers were hoping he'd be able to score the goals that would help keep them up in the old division one. In the remainder of his time at the club, which lasted eight more years and took him well into his mid-30s, Booth experienced two play-off semi-final losses, one relegation and one promotion, retiring as the club's third highest ever goalscorer and with the fourth highest ever appearances. He remains at the club to this day in an ambassadorial capacity, working within the community to keep Huddersfield Town as connected as possible to those who support them.

It hasn't just been on the field where Huddersfield were struggling until recently, either. While the relegations and period at the basement of English football were bad, there was a time where their finances were worse, and administration became a serious threat. Having overspent and pushed their limits in hope of securing promotion to the Premier League, debts of almost £20m crippled the club in March of 2003 when they had failed to do so, and with nobody looking to take the club over in such a sorry state, liquidation was not out of the question. Players and staff had spent four to five months working without pay when Ken Davy, who owns the Huddersfield Giants, stepped in at the eleventh hour to keep the club afloat - but there were concerns over how shares regarding the ownership of the stadium were being handled. According to the administrators, Davy only paid £2 for the stadium shares, which he would then combine with those he owned as chairman of the Giants, and ring-fence them in a separate company, effectively making him the sole majority owner of the stadium.

Both the rugby league team and Town needed new homes, with Leeds Road at the brink of disrepair and the Giants already sharing it after their Fartown Ground became unfit for purpose. It was a move that benefitted not only both parties, but the area as a whole. Regenerating that part of the town, it was a council funded project that would have health and fitness purposes away from the sports teams. The design, too, remains unique and celebrated, with the architects winning awards for how forward thinking the ground was, especially with so many functions to cater for. While it was originally envisaged that the creation of a new state-of-the-art stadium in 1994 would be there for football, rugby league and community use, the issue regarding the shares left a cloud over the ground for many years. Before their administration, Town owned 40% of the shares, as did the local council, with the rugby league club owning the other 20%, but by the time Davy had rescued the club, he had 60% of the stadium to himself, which fans believed was stopping the football team from progressing as they should, and threatened their future. By his own admission, Davy believed that was what was owed to him, after the personal risk he'd taken to keep Huddersfield Town solvent. Until the arrival of lifelong fan Dean Hoyle as chairman elect in 2008, it caused a rift between the ownership and fan base, promoting several demonstrations and protests.

Originally joining the board in April 2008, it took Hoyle just over a year to take over as both chairman and majority shareholder in June 2009. Having founded the greeting card chain Card Factory alongside his wife Janet in 1997, Hoyle grew the company over the next decade, meaning by 2009, the firm had over 500 stores and employed more than 5,000 people. Selling the company in 2010 to a venture capitalist firm, industry reporters suggested the final fee was north of £350m, leaving Hoyle free to take over as chairman of Huddersfield Town, with more than enough money behind him to match the ambition he had for the club. It wasn't until 2013, however, that Hoyle managed to secure the shares back from Davy, with the club paying a nominal £1 to do so, with Hoyle personally repaying £2m worth of loans directly to Davy in order to secure the club their stake in the stadium.

Setting up a charitable trust to guard the shares from any future owner or board of Huddersfield Town, it was one of many early defining acts that sold Huddersfield fans on Hoyle, most of whom had understandably come to be somewhat wary of owners by that point. He was, and remains, one of the main catalysts for Huddersfield Town turning their fortunes around, and that was more down to how he talked about the club, than the money he spent on it. He had the passion of a fan but with the confidence of a man who'd made himself a multi-millionaire, and that was infectious. Town were a club who'd been without that level of affection at that level for some time, and seeing somebody care about the club again, and talk about them taking them forward with real passion was enough to spark a somewhat overdue renewal of hope. Installing an exciting young manager in charge in Lee Clark and backing his man by overhauling the squad, the 2009-2010 season was a fresh start for the club, but ultimately ended in disappointment, losing in the play-off semi-finals to Millwall after finishing sixth in the league. The following season, Town finished five points shy of automatic promotion, eventually losing in the play-off final at Old Trafford to Peterborough 3-0.

They would finally be promoted to the Championship one season later, but only after Lee Clark had been relieved of his duties and replaced by Simon Grayson, who had a track record of gaining promotion through that division. Finishing fourth in the league, Town overcame Milton Keynes in the play-off semi-finals, before defeating Sheffield United 8-7 on penalties, after drawing 0-0 after added time. Grayson was replaced by Mark Robins during their first year back in the Championship, and the club narrowly avoided relegation, finishing 19th. The following season, Robins led Town to a 17th placed finish, but was quickly let go the following season, with Chris Powell guiding the club to a 16th placed finish having taken his place.

In a similar pattern as those that came before him, Chris Powell only lasted until the 4th of November, barely four months into the 2015-2016 season. By that time, Huddersfield had only won three league matches all season, amassing just 15 points in 15 games, leaving them precariously close to the relegation places.

The following day at 1.30pm, on the 5th of November 2015, Huddersfield Town confirmed that David Wagner had been appointed the club's new head coach.

CHAPTER ONE:

REVOLUTION

"Shall I tell you what happened?"

Huddersfield Town owner and chairman Dean Hoyle is sitting in a heritage themed hospitality suite at one end of the John Smith's Stadium, telling the tale of how David Wagner came to be head coach.

"It's as simple as this: when Stuart Webber said to me, 'I've had a call from an agent, we've got the chance of getting Jurgen Klopp's number two in from Dortmund', I went pffft - I like the sound of that! That's it. Football is an entertainment industry isn't it?"

While there was some speculation that Huddersfield had as a club made a conscious decision to go in a different direction and headhunted Wagner from the second team at Borussia Dortmund, the truth of the matter is far less romantic - it was just a call from an agent to a director of football who was lucky enough to have a chairman willing to take a risk. When that version of events is put to Hoyle, he laughs it off. He does that a fair bit, to be honest. "It isn't rocket science", he says, shrugging his shoulders.

"I remember a friend of mine texted me when we appointed him and he said to me, 'He could be the chosen one'. I'm like, he hasn't seen him play! He hasn't even seen an interview, but it was just that unknown quantity.

"It's like when you sign a footballer, if you sign Billy Bloggs from Iran, Kazakhstan, Canada or Brazil, you might think woof, he's exciting! Or you might think you're going to sign a player from Middlesbrough and think hmm, he's a bit dire. Sometimes the unknown is really exciting."

At this point, Hoyle has only been asked one question, but he knows the story he's been asked for, and he's delivering it breathlessly, like you imagine you might if you were reminding people how you found a jackpot winning lottery ticket down the back of your sofa.

"When I got in front of David for the first time," he continues, "and he talked to me about how his teams have to be the fittest because of the style they'll be playing, I'm suddenly thinking, we aren't as fit as what we should be, and we haven't been for years. So straight away, fitness it is then.

"When he came over and described to us about the way he played his football, what he does in training and his philosophy, in a very simple way, I could just understand it, and what he was trying to get across. I kind of liked him, he had the right personality, he were German - win, win! It all came together there and then. What David did different here is that when he first came on board, he did everything he said he was going to do in the interview, and that is really unique because I've met enough football managers to know that it doesn't happen often."

It speaks volumes of the man that, when asked about his own arrival at the club in an official capacity, he seeks to play it down, and all that excitement that's present when he's reliving the arrival of David Wagner makes way for a far more measured and muted response. The way he describes his takeover is one of reluctance, but in the knowledge that without change, Huddersfield weren't going to be getting out of League One anytime soon.

"I quickly did the deal with Ken Davy to initially come and be an investor, not the chairman, so that I could put a few quid - he could carry on as chairman. I was busy with Card Factory at that point, and I didn't particularly want the profile. I went on holiday to Tenerife and at that point, I said to my wife Janet, I'm not going to take over, I'm not doing it, I'm not interested.

"But when I came home and I went to a game, it was absolutely dire against Southend and I thought to myself, I've got to do something, but at the same time, I knew I couldn't work with Ken - the difference in culture and difference in ages was too much. I decided that if I was going to get involved with Huddersfield, I would take it on 100% - all I wanted to do initially was put smiles on people's faces and get them to the Championship, which

I knew I had the finances to do. Getting them to the Premier League though, different ball game."

Given the issues with the stadium shares, the relative lack of investment and general sense of inertia that had set in across the place, Huddersfield Town began to exist just for the sake of it. There was no real ambition to improve themselves, but enough teams struggling around them to ensure fairly comfortable mid-table finishes in the third tier, year in year out. That was something Hoyle was keen to change from day one of his tenure in charge.

"The club had no clear direction at that stage, but to be honest, the same can be said about myself. When I took over we had a handful of decent years and got to the Championship - then we probably had two or three years of what one would call, little ambition. We had Simon Grayson, Mark Robins and Chris Powell in charge in quick succession. If I sold the club tomorrow, one would look back on those times and think, they were also very poor. Football cannot always be on an upward trajectory, sometimes you've got to balance out, reflect and those aren't good times, but I would say your success in life is as much based on your failures as anything else.

"My darkest hour as chairman of the club was Chris Powell's reign - it's the reason we got David Wagner in - because if Chris had done well, then I wouldn't have gone so far left field as I did with Wagner, because let's be fair, he was left field. I mean, really, where on earth did that come from? It was so radical, but I knew I just couldn't carry on. I always have this saying: if things are shit, you throw the hand grenade in and there's one thing for sure, it may get better or it may get worse, but it definitely won't be the same. So that's what I did. Luckily, it looks a lot better from where I'm sitting."

While it was a big change and risk for Huddersfield in hiring Wagner, the first foreign manager in the history of the club, it was an equally large leap of faith from the man himself, who was entering his first role as head coach of a first team in a league, area and environment he was a complete and utter alien to - and at first, he had his own set of doubts.

"To be honest," says David Wagner, crossing one leg over the other, sitting in an armchair at the corner of his office, "I was a little bit disappointed." He catches himself at this point, and decides to rephrase, perhaps of the opinion that 'disappointed' is a tad stronger than he wants to be.

"I had a different expectation from my experience in Germany," he continues, happier having found a more political way around the point he was trying to make. From having worked at Borussia Dortmund, one of the richest and more forward thinking clubs in the world, it was somewhat of a shock to see how Huddersfield were operating before his arrival. "I had different ideas about how a football club should be structured and organised in terms of the facilities and everything to do with the football side of business, like training and fitness. Huddersfield had already been a Championship club for a number of years before I arrived, but when I compared what we had here with the clubs in Germany in a similar position, it was different. Usually, the environment on the football side is of a higher standard, I would say."

Far from love at first site, Wagner set about changing the entire landscape of the training complex on arrival, pushing for a higher standard of facility and privacy, which hadn't previously been a priority. Canalside, the base of Town's training operations, is open to the public. The home to a bridge club, bowling green, snooker hall, and gym, it's the sort of place you can drive up to at will and get a pint without being bothered, once. Something that Dean Hoyle is keen on maintaining, he believes having the public at close quarters keeps the club honest, a trait he's determined not to let slip away with any ease.

That continued relationship with the public and access granted to them is clearly a point of pride for the club. They like being different - not just for the sake of it, but because it's quirks like that which can contribute to on-field success. When you don't have the world's biggest budget and you aren't a side blessed with stars from one through eleven, you have to find other ways of securing marginal gains. It's certainly an area of focus for the media and communications department.

"Educating the real national influencers in what makes Huddersfield Town Huddersfield Town is the next step for us. For example, we get people like Gary Lineker turning up to Canalside now, and he's obviously one of the biggest names in English football as far as the media side is concerned, if not the biggest. I can tell you with certainty that he's not visited here in the last twelve years in the same period I've worked here, and I understand that.

"But when he comes here and we bring him into the training ground - immediately as you walk in there are people here just going about their day. He looked really confused and was a bit like, 'who are they?' I had to explain that they're just members of the general public from our town, either getting some food and drink, or getting involved with one of the social or sporting clubs we house here. For example, on a Tuesday morning, we've a bridge club playing here. They're here every week, and have been for time.

"You get these people down who cover football nationally and they're forever asking where's the fence at the end of the drive? Or they point to some people in the cafeteria and ask what they do within the club, and I sort of laugh and say, I think they've just come for lunch. One guy once walked through with his mouth agape and went 'there's a crown green bowling team outside!' And we were sort of like yeah, there is. There are also guys playing snooker in the other room - that's an average day for us.

"It's not until they come here that they start to actually learn about what makes us who we are, and that we embrace the community coming here and being a part of it, rather than locking ourselves away. Just recently, we held an annual fireworks display, and there's just David Wagner with his family just milling around the thing. If you didn't know who he was, he'd just look like another member of the public who'd come down to enjoy the event. You don't get that anywhere else. We've somehow managed to mix elite sport with having a fully stocked bar - and that's pretty special.

"For me, it's been so interesting to see what people from outside the club pick up on the most, and what gets their imaginations going. When people started writing about Town who hadn't been here before, half the time they ended up highlighting stuff that wasn't even to do with the football - that's really heartwarming for a club like ours. Our foundation, for example, is something that really seemed to grab folk who weren't aware of the work we did in the community. I know every club has a charity these days, but they've not served almost a million breakfasts to little kids in the local area - so when somebody hears that for the first time, they're pretty taken aback.

"It's one thing to hear about what a club does in the local area, and be told how the players are with the public, but it's something else entirely to be part of that, and to see it first-hand. It's those things that actually make us different, and unique as a club."

For the new coach, however, it wasn't ideal having the general public able to keep a watch on training during their lunch break with a fag on the go, or his players having to wait to use gym equipment, because some old dear hadn't quite finished her ten-minute workout on the exercise bike yet. Located to the rear of the facility was a large, steel enclosure, which was in essence a shed, but a completely permanent structure. In use as somewhere for the groundsmen to keep their equipment, it was quickly converted into a gym area and office space, creating a more professional environment for the players and coaching staff to exist in. Wagner doesn't dispute the need for a community club like Town to keep close to their public, but when it's time to think about football, he says, there needn't be any distractions.

There's even a fence surrounding the pitches the first team train on now, which hadn't been the case previously. With changes to the infrastructure being made, Wagner then turned his attention to overhauling the training habits of the club, and improving the breadth of his support staff.

"In terms of the training schedule," Wagner says, leaning forward in his seat slightly, folding one hand on top of the other, "this is the usual amount of work in Germany. There is Sunday morning training, before double sessions on Monday, Tuesday and Wednesday. Then we start training to match the time our next game will be kicking off on the Thursday and Friday, so either in the afternoon or evening. This is usual in Germany, I think. I grew up with that kind of schedule as a youth player, and it continued as a professional. It's not unreasonable to expect your squad to become fitter if you start training seven or eight times a week rather than four or five.

"All the other things we changed step by step. We changed the nutrition of the players and brought in a chef, moved the gym and the offices - we now have our own professional environment rather than having everything combined with the community. I like having the combination, it's unique to our football club, but now we can practise professional football in an area which we made sure is of a professional standard.

"At the beginning we had croquet on the training pitch where there was only a mark between them and us. There wasn't even a fence between them and us so they were playing croquet while we were playing football. We even shared our gym with the community at the start, but this isn't the professional standard that you have to have and this was what we changed, step by step. We hired additional man power in terms of recovery, physios, and head of performance - even little things like a sauna. Everything that we brought to this football club is of the standard that we needed if we wanted to be as professional as possible."

By coincidence, Wagner's first week at the club coincided with an international break, so the team took themselves away to Marbella for a week of warm weather training - with their families in tow. It was one of many early questions the new coach asked of his chairman, but Hoyle wasn't fazed by his new man's demands.

"If they're reasonable ideas, we try to go there," Hoyle says. "He's very demanding, but he backs it all up. He said to me before that trip, 'I've just spoken to Jurgen, and Jurgen said that the best thing he's done at Liverpool is taken all the players - with the wives and the families - to Dubai. I want to do it too, I want to go to Marbella.'

"My first question is obviously, well how much is it going to cost, David? £100,000 - bloody hell, that's a lot of money! But I can assure you now, part of success has been taking all the players, the wives, the children, all to Marbella and the reason is - there was philosophy behind it - you're not just going for a lads weekend away.

"The philosophy and mentality behind it was quite simple: he wanted the players to feel responsible individually for other people's families so that when they're on the pitch, it's not just about them as footballers, it's about, if they make a mistake or they can try and put 10% harder work in, the influence and the difference it will make to other people's lives, they take responsibility. When they all started socialising, it was more of a team unit and I think that shone through. That collectively and individual responsibility. There's method where there's madness, without question."

That early trip to Marbella wasn't a holiday, but a boot camp - it was just an added bonus that the families had been invited along. Town's captain at the time, Mark Hudson (who now makes up part of Wagner's coaching staff) was one of the club's longer serving players at the time, and cottoned on to how different their new head coach was fairly quickly, with that week away proving the foundation for everything that was to follow.

"For me, the difference was immediate. The level of detail, for him to be able to get these ideas across to us within the first few days was really impressive. He took us away to Marbella and in a way, he broke down his plan for what we were going to do for the rest of the season. We even spent some time in the classroom before we actually went on the grass. He didn't give us too much each time to pick up on, giving us a bit of detail and theory here and there, before going outside and putting that into action. We'd have a break and do the same again, only with a little bit more detail on what we were going to do on the pitch, then we went on the pitch and worked through it again.

"It was a bit like being back at school, with him stood in front of the board at the front. He had loads of video clips, so there were clear reasons why we were going to do each specific drill - everything had a purpose and an end goal, designed to make us better for having been through it. That's where and how he created our identity from the word go, from that first week.

"I've never experienced another coach doing that in my career, and I'd been playing professionally for comfortably over a decade by that point, perhaps even closer to two. Obviously managers do things differently and managers do have other competing philosophies, ideas, and identity - but for him to come into a new club and adopt a group that was already there that you can't change and to give us as players a structure for what we were going to do and how we were going to do it and maintain it, it was second to none."

It wasn't just the the players who had picked up on how different life was going to be under Wagner, but the staff at the club - most of whom have been there for some years - were noticing the energy and direction that the new coach had brought with him. David Threlfall-Sykes, the head of media and communications at Town, joined the club straight out of university in 2005 on a temporary contract in a junior role, and hasn't left since. David Wagner is the eighth permanent head coach he's seen in his time working for the club - not counting various caretakers - yet still, that trip to Marbella managed to surprise even him.

"The managers I've worked with in the past, they've all

had their own nuances, but the basics of what they do is fairly similar. They all come in and train at half ten in the morning and the majority of the players are away by one in the afternoon, with the manager usually staying a little longer. The training sessions themselves didn't tend to vary loads from coach to coach, and then David comes in, and I remember him in Marbella stopping sessions for really detailed stuff.

"They were doing these passing drills with mannequins, and him and Christoph Buhler are stopping the sessions because the passes weren't quite right. I'm talking detailed stuff, like safe side and difficult side, and there was a real emphasis on getting the real small details right, which to me as someone who's been in football long enough and seen a lot of training, you thought, this is different, and there wasn't any of the stuff that you were used to seeing. It piqued my attention and I'm surrounded by it every day, so I knew that it would pique people's attention outside the club, because this was different.

"Saying that, though, I think as good a coach as David clearly is, you should never underplay just how clever a bloke he is as well. Aside from the football management side of it, he's just a very astute man, especially when you consider that a lot of the time, he's not communicating in his first language. His attention to detail and his savviness when it comes to timing and knowing what to say is quite incredible. One of David's biggest strengths, whether it's with the media or with the players, is his ability to get a quite complex message over in a very simple, understandable way. That's why when the players go out on the pitch, they all know exactly what their job is and that's why he's so good when he's speaking to the press, too. He's the type of bloke that's always one step ahead."

Away from football, it wasn't lost on the staff how important that bonding experience was, not just for the team as professional footballers, but for everybody's families to get to know one another. That was what helped breed their supreme togetherness. Andy Brook, the club kitman who's worked at the club his entire life - first as an occasional labourer, then as painter and decorator, before eventually being handed kitman duties by Steve Bruce during his time as manager of the club - went along with his young family, speaks about the afternoons the players and staff spent together with great fondness, as it was a level of intimacy he'd never before experienced during his time in football.

"When we went to Marbella," he says, twiddling his feet off the side of a bench in the home dressing room at the John Smith's Stadium, his tracksuit freshly printed with his initials, "I remember we trained in the morning and the afternoon you were with your family. We were all sat on the beach together playing football, the kids were running in the sea and that, all the players' wives together, there were no segregation. I think that's what the boss wanted - we were all together, the kids would run out together, they were all playing together. But there wouldn't be a table where people sat on their own. The whole week for all five nights, we sat in a different place at the table for dinner, that's how laid back and familiar we became. Everyone got so close, my kids loved it."

When football teams discuss intangible factors like spirit, there is a worry that they can come off sounding a bit more cheesy than they'd like. This sport isn't shy of a few David Brent-like characters, so when there are discussions regarding mood, feeling and unity, it can feel somewhat hollow and awkward if they don't appear to be accompanied with the requisite amount of sincerity. It's one step removed from a bad Apprentice audition tape, where someone in a loud suit reels off buzzwords like 'synergy' - but that hasn't ever been the case at Huddersfield, even from the outside looking in. Finding the right balance of emotion and action was central to life under David Wagner getting off to the best possible start.

"Togetherness has been key for the club since David came in," David Threlfall-Sykes will later tell me. "That first Marbella trip is a perfect example - it was an idea from the coach, and then the chairman backed him to do it. We took the families out with us, and we haven't done that before. It was such a nice little touch, because David was insistent, make sure you bring your partner, and bring your kids. He wanted to make sure that they felt a real part of it as well. I remember David making a special point of saying to them: 'This is our way of saying thank you. We train, play and travel a lot and I know you don't see them as much as you'd like'. It was a really smart and innovative way to get everybody as invested as possible in the success of the team and the club. I don't think we can ignore the significance of that."

Given how profoundly those early days and weeks after

David Wagner joined the club are looked back on, and just how quickly all involved were about to get on the same page and set the ball rolling for what was to come, results for the rest of the season didn't really reflect that same level of positivity - but the performances did. In his first game in charge, Wagner took Town to Sheffield Wednesday in a Yorkshire derby, and for large periods they played the high-flying Owls off the field. Going one nil up, it was only in the latter stages, when the Terriers were tiring - not yet as fit as they needed to be - that the home side were able to make the game look far more comfortable than it was, winning 3-1.

In their first home game, it was a similar story. Playing against a strong and heavily invested Middlesbrough side - who were at the time the best team in the division, eventually going up automatically in second place - Town pressed their opponents off the park, looked by far the brighter and more dangerous side, but still fell to a 2-0 loss, with the visitors scoring with their only two shots on target during the entire game. Despite losing, Huddersfield were clapped off the field, with fans aware that what they had seen wasn't fairly reflected in the final scoreline. Within two matches, hope had been restored where previously there had been a vacuum. The highlight of those first six months, a 4-1 away win at Elland Road against Leeds, just underlined what everybody was beginning to learn about Huddersfield's new outlook on how to play the game. Despite missing an early penalty and falling a goal down afterwards, Town managed to level before the end of the half, and then scored three goals within eight minutes midway through the second half to put the game well beyond their West Yorkshire rivals.

That game had all the hallmarks of what Wagner had been preaching since he arrived at the club, and things couldn't have clicked in to place at a better time. Town were restless without the ball, cutting off passing lanes, chasing down possession in packs, winning anything that was even vaguely loose and making Leeds pay for their mistakes. While there had been hints in bits and pieces of play, this was the first time the side had really strung together enough of those moments to make it matter in a tangible sense. At the full-time whistle, David Wagner made his way over to the corner of Elland Road where the Town fans stood and punched the air with all the ferocity of a man trying to somehow knockout the wind. If there wasn't a connection between the manager and the fan base before - there certainly was now.

Finishing the season in 19th position, just three places and 11 points above the relegation zone, Town's record under Wagner in the league was still far from impressive on paper come the end of the season. In his 30 league matches in charge, Town won just ten games, lost on fourteen occasions, and drew six times. However, given that Wagner was operating with somebody else's squad, performances were rightly prioritised over position, and the club ended the season on a positive note, content with how their season had gone since changing manager. David Wagner had given Huddersfield something they lacked for some time - a team to cheer for, and something to believe in. That would prove crucial in the months to come.

CHAPTER TWO:

E—I-E-I-E-I-O . . .

To characterise the summer of 2016 as a busy time for Huddersfield Town would be somewhat of an understatement. Not letting their positive momentum from the previous season slide, they did their business early, completely overhauling their squad as quickly as possible, with many of their biggest deals done before the transfer window had even been officially opened. A clear sign of their intent and excitement for what was to come, that was matched by the mood from the fan base, too, who were delirious at the sight of their club finally appearing to have a real go at the season, rather than maximising their ambitions at avoiding relegation.

In total, fourteen players were allowed to leave the club on a permanent basis, with a further four going out on loan. In their place, Town signed eleven new players on a permanent basis, with four more joining on a loan basis. An emphatic vote of confidence in David Wagner, there could be no accusations that the club weren't doing everything within their power to give their head coach everything he needed to get the very best out of the season. Twelve of the permanent departures and two of the players leaving on loan were ratified on July 1st, the official opening of the transfer window, while nine permanent transfers in and one of the loan signings were also made official on the same day. Huddersfield would formally do more business on that one day than they would go on to do in the remainder of the transfer window.

To underline just how well planned their transfer business was, though, it's worth factoring their budget – the fourth lowest in the Championship that season. Relying on the loan market and making four free signings, their largest fee paid out was for central defender Christopher Schindler from 1860 Munich, who arrived for a then club record £1.8 million. Having taken a fee in the region of £1.2 million for Joel Lynch from Queens Park Rangers, the majority of the Schindler fee was already covered, with Town effectively using that sale to fund their purchase, like an elaborate part exchange.

Even when they were spending money, they were doing so incredibly wisely.

As well as Schindler, the players joining Town were young goalkeepers Luke Coddington, Joel Coleman and George Dorrington, from Middlesbrough, Oldham Athletic and Manchester United respectively. There were two further additions in central defence, with Michael Hefele coming from Dynamo Dresden, and David Wagner returning to his old club to bring Jon Gorenc Stankovic from the Dortmund second team. In the left-back department, Christopher Lowe joined from Kaiserslautern and younger Tareiq Holmes-Dennis made his way up from Charlton, while defensive midfielder Ivan Paurevic joined from Russian outfit FC Ufa, but had crossed paths with Wagner in their Dortmund days. Jack Payne, a young attacking midfielder from Southend joined after Town agreed to pay his hometown club compensation, with Dutch winger Rajiv van La Parra rounding off the permanent summer signings, having originally come to the club on loan from Wolves the season before, with an option to buy.

Arriving on loan, Elias Kachunga came from FC Ingolstadt with an option to buy, while goalkeeper Danny

Ward came across from Liverpool, seeking first team opportunities. Exciting attacking midfield option Kasey Palmer came from Chelsea, while Australian national team star Aaron Mooy was offered to Huddersfield for the season by Manchester City, who identified the Terriers as an ideal place for their player to develop.

One theme that became prevalent amongst those joining the club were their previous roles at the club they left to join Huddersfield - many of them had been captain, and it was too many to be a coincidence. Speaking to David Wagner about that, it's clear it's something they spent some time identifying, too.

"We searched for captains but, more importantly, we searched for captains who were foreign. I thought if someone is a captain at a German club, he knows exactly what he has to do right, what mistakes not to make, and if we bring other players from abroad in to the country, they can be more involved in trying to integrate their fellow foreigner, because it's something they will have already been through.

"On top of that, I wanted to have players who played more

at the top of the table in the competition they had come from than the bottom - this is why Michael Hefele arrived, who got promoted with Dresden, Chris Lowe who got promoted and won the league with Dortmund - they would have the right habits and experience for what we were trying to do. They didn't have to be league winners or get promotion before, but they needn't to know what the top of the league was like. If possible, we wanted to get that type of player in and because of our small budget, we went into the loan market for very young, inexperienced players who looked ready for senior football, like Kasey Palmer, Izzy Brown, even Danny Ward only played one season previously. It was largely dictated by the size of our budget and because of our knowledge in the German market. It was the route that made the most sense to us."

These weren't the household names at the time that they would go on to become, and given that Huddersfield's transfer activity had centred around known and proven qualities until then, how was it for Dean Hoyle, as chairman, to fund moves for players he may never have even heard of previously? What was it like, having already made a leap of faith to hire a manager, to do so again with a completely revised approach to the transfer market?

"There's got to be trust," Hoyle offers, matter-of-factly. "For example, David comes up with Schindler, so Stuart Webber goes out to watch him in Munich, and meets the player. Schindler then comes over here, has a look around, watches training, goes to the stadium - and then we decided to pay for the record fee. It was a lot of money. It's literally just down to trust, though, you have to trust other people's judgements. I have to trust people within the club, I've got to trust the coach and the scout, so when they all say collectively that's the man we should go for, you have to go with it. It's as simple as that."

Hoyle remains hands-on with how he handles transfers, perhaps a hangover from having built his own company from scratch - he's not gone far wrong in life when he's been the one dotting the i's and crossing the t's. So much so that, when it's put to him how many of the transfers pass through his desk, he half scoffs his reply.

"Every one! Because ultimately, it's my cash. They all come past me. Sometimes I'll say, where's he going to play? Sometimes I'll knock them back and say - quite frankly - what's the point of having the fourth choice here? What's going to happen to choice one, two and three then? Where and when is he actually going to play? Managers don't always get it right. I think its about operating as a collective. It's not about one individual, it's about collective responsibility. That's why Ross Wilson did well here, that's why Stuart Webber did well here."

It's important to note at this point that, where the football club are concerned, Hoyle isn't always this measured. Anybody who has had the pleasure of sitting within the vicinity of him on a match day will tell you he remains just as passionate as a fan as he always has been, and juggling his responsibility as chairman comes in tandem with that. When asked about that balance, between being a fan and acting like the boss, he cops to having gotten carried away in the past, and making mistakes he ought not to have done. In his early 40s when he took over the club with no previous experience in being an owner, there was always going to have been a learning curve.

"You know what?" he replies, with half a smirk appearing on his face as he reminisces, "I have got carried away sometimes, yeah - especially on the wages you pay or the players you buy, not particularly now but more in the past. In the Lee Clark days, he had this mantra, kid in a sweet shop. His solution - a great guy by the way - but his solution to problems would just be to get a new player. I quickly came round to it, because I thought they started performing better when less players are coming in. I'll always remember a player, Sean Morrison, he's now at Cardiff - a centre back. We could have signed him for £250,000 from Swindon, and we really did nearly have him, but Lee was going through a really tough patch, he had too many players and I said no, no more players. Well, actually, in hindsight, I should have signed him because he's a great player - but you win some and you lose some, and in that you do realise how to manage people, no two ways about it. I have to manage the coaches, the managers and then they manage the players. That's how it works."

Capitalising on the increased interest in the club across the town and surrounding areas, the commercial department rolled out a new season ticket scheme, completely restructuring what had come before it. Aiming to make supporting the club more affordable, adult and senior season tickets would cost just £179, which worked out at less than £8 per game. Children aged 8-17 would have to pay just £69 for their seat, while under-8s would cost just £23 for the year. The marketing that accompanied the season tickets previewed the season as the 'Wagner Revolution', with Town's head coach taking a starring role in all promotional material. The scheme, which was fully backed by Dean Hoyle, was an undoubted success, with the club selling over 15,000 before a ball had even been kicked.

One of the main forces behind the campaign was commercial director Sean Jarvis, who has spent the majority of him time at the club attempting to make Huddersfield Town an invaluable part of not only the local community where the fans are concerned, but the business community, as well. Constantly working to open new doors for the club via commercial partnerships and increased exposure, he looks the part for that sort of role - never seen in anything but a well tailored suit, with cropped haircut styled purposefully to one side and a well kempt beard to boot, he could happily pass for an extra in Mad Men.

"It was an interesting one," he says, having been asked if there was some risk attached to designing a season ticket campaign around a coach who could up and leave without a second's notice. "I remember the board meeting. We were all sat around, and we knew that David had potential. You could see that in that prior season. We went, what is it the fan base are connecting with at this moment in time around the season campaign? Our initial thoughts were along the lines of Huddersfield Town being part of Huddersfield as a town, and I personally remember going, they're not connecting with us at this moment in time, they're connecting with David Wagner.

"We went Wagner Revolution, because it is a revolution. That's what is happening here. We were all nervous in the board meeting because you are, you're pinning the campaign around that one individual and that could have gone pear-shaped, but we felt it struck a chord with everyone here, it then engaged that fan base and with the man who has to make the decisions on the pitch. So we thought, let's go for it. It soon caught on. It connected. You could see people talked about the Wagner Revolution, but then there was always that danger that you put the man on the pedestal. We had the following board room meeting and we thought, we have to be careful here. David will decide his future if he's successful, if he gets approached - which he has been - we need to connect it back to the club.

"It's a bit like a graphic equaliser. At that point, we'd put up Wagner and that worked, but you can't keep doing that because then what if Wagner disappears? He gets sacked, or he goes to another job. That happens in football. The rest is lost. So now, there's arguably less of Wagner, even though he's very popular, there's a bit more Terrier Spirit. There's a bit more Terrier dog, the identity around that, who we are as a football club. So we've actually increased the Terrier Spirit, increased our identity through this other bit of the graphic equaliser, so Wagner's come down a bit and the others maybe have gone up, so it's creating that right kind of balance.

"Make no mistakes though, David is a catalyst to it - but he's the employee of the club, like any football club. Alex Ferguson is Manchester United, Pochettino is the same at Spurs - they are high profile figures, but it's finding that balance whereby when that figure disappears, you don't lose the heart of your club, and that's where we have to get to."

With such a high level of transfer activity making so many headlines, and that many more people than usual being given a chance to go and see Huddersfield play, the appetite to follow the club was higher than it had been for some years. Not even based on success, which was still far from guaranteed, the fact that the football club appeared to have finally woken from a slumber and looked to engage with people in a proactive way caught the imagination in a way they had failed to previously. While there is plenty of credit due to David Wagner for being the type of character that could provoke that kind of response, not every football club would respond to that by lowering ticket prices. The master stroke, making the matches so cheap for children and teenagers to attend, gave the club access to a generation they may have otherwise missed out on, securing the future supporters of the football club.

What it all also demonstrated was how much trust there was between Dean Hoyle and David Wagner, because the club had gone all out in both a footballing and commercial capacity for their head coach. Given the way coaches come and go from football clubs in this day and age, there's an immense amount of risk in placing an entire season ticket campaign on the shoulders of one man, but given that both he and his assistant Christoph Buhler had just signed new improved deals that summer, there was a confidence that Town were safe in doing so, at least for the immediate future. Having been backed so fully in the transfer market, many believed there was no reason for Wagner to be tempted elsewhere, especially given the connection he appeared to have made with both the club and the fan base.

There was, however, a fear that Huddersfield may fall victim of trying to do too much too soon, with many predicting a slow start given how drastically the squad had been turned over. With the club having so many different nationalities in the same dressing room, it isn't unheard of that teething problems occur and gelling the team can take longer than expected - but to tackle this, David Wagner already had a plan. With so many of his core squad already signed and together, Town began their pre-season with a trip to Sweden, but rather than train, they were going to live in the wild together, with no modern amenities to fall back on. Players were forced to abandon their mobile phones and their electrical gadgets, and stayed in an area with not so much as a bed or a toilet nearby.

Andy Brook, the club's kitman, remembers being asked to get the equipment ready for the trip, because each player was going to be sent to him individually to pick up what they needed to pack.

"The boss came and told me what he was planning, so I asked for a list of what kit he wanted packing. He said right, so we need kits, we need a cup, we need leggings ... loads of different weird stuff like baseball caps and I'm thinking where are they actually going? Then he told the lads to come and see me and I did the kit, got it ready for them to collect, and there was some weird stuff in there. Big coats and all sorts, stuff that you wouldn't expect in pre-season training, especially when they're so used to going away to train in warm weather. I wasn't there, luckily, but it did make them closer and stronger for definite, you could see that when they came back."

Staying for four days, the trip was designed to bond the team away from football, with the squad constantly rotating who they were partnered with for activities and tasks, forced to communicate and become aware of one another in ways that, without that trip, they may not have ever experienced. Fetching their own fire wood, sharing tents, paddling for fresh water - it was the type of trip that formed the basis of what would become known as their Terrier identity. There was a training camp in Austria that followed, but far more orthodox than the first, with friendlies taking place and the squad being put through its paces across three sessions per day. If the regular training schedule under Wagner seemed like intense work, pre-season took that up yet another gear or two, especially in the warmer weather.

Come the opening day of the season, it was clear whatever Huddersfield had been doing was paying off. Playing against Brentford - who'd come to the John Smith's on the last day of the previous season, rolling Town over 5-1 with relative ease - it was an ideal opportunity to show just how far they'd come from the end of last season to the start of this one. Taking the lead through Elias Kachunga after dominating for the majority of the match, Town let themselves down by allowing Brentford to equalise against the run of play in the 77th minute. Reacting to the goal, David Wagner brought on Kasey Palmer for Jack Payne, and within a minute of making his debut, Palmer was scoring Town's winner with his first touch of the game, wheeling away to embrace Wagner as he celebrated.

18,479 were in attendance on the opening day for Huddersfield, the side's highest attendance on an opening day for 46 years. Town then followed that result up by going to St James' Park and beating newly relegated Newcastle United 2-1, with Nahki Wells and

Jack Payne scoring either side of a Dwight Gayle equaliser, the winner not arriving until inside the final ten minutes. Three days later, Huddersfield were at their second away game at a side who'd just dropped out of the Premier League, with Aston Villa taking less than half an hour to move into the lead. With the match looking to be heading for a narrow 1-0 Villa win, David Wagner threw German central defender Michael Hefele on in an attacking role in the 86th minute, and within seconds of entering the field of play, he chased down Pierluigi Gollini in the Villa goal, who was making a routine clearance.

Rather than booting the ball away, however, the Villa keeper hoofed the ball straight against Michael Hefele's oncoming backside, with the defender-turned-forward having leaped to block his clearance. Gollini unable to do anything but look on, the ball bounced straight off Hefele and straight into the goal, giving Town an improbable point in a match where they had looked destined to lose.

Continuing their run of scoring late winners in their next match against Barnsley at home, Chris Lowe had his fantastic strike cancelled out by Alfie Mawson, the match still drawn 1-1 well past the 90th minute. However, with virtually the last kick of the game, Town played their way up the field, before the ball fell to defensive midfielder Jonathan Hogg, who'd inexplicably found himself in space inside the area. Side-footing the ball into the roof of the net in the 92nd minute as only somebody who doesn't shoot all that often can, that win took Town top of the Championship table, somewhere they'd briefly been after the second game of the season.

To round out August, an early goal at home inside ten minutes from Rajiv van La Parra against his former side Wolves was enough to finish the month undefeated, having won four league games from five, drawing the other. Huddersfield finished the first month of the season clear at the top of the Championship, leaving many who'd expected them to struggle dumbfounded as to how they found themselves in such a position.

CHAPTER THREE:

TOP OF THE LEAGUE

With an international break falling immediately after the Wolves win, Huddersfield had the chance to stay at the summit of the Championship for an extended period. David Wagner was also able to get the majority of his side back on the training field and ensure they remained as fit and sharp as possible. As part of their preparations, Town played and won a behind-closed-doors training ground friendly against Liverpool at the invitation of Jurgen Klopp, with the Reds fielding their selection of first team players that weren't on international duty.

That proved to be an ideal manner in which to get up to speed ahead of a massive game away to Leeds, which held extra significance for both sides beyond the obvious - should Huddersfield win, they would remain top, but if Leeds were to lose they could find themselves dangerously close to the relegation zone, with Garry Monk's job already being brought into question.

Having been to Elland Road midway through the previous season and left 4-1 winners, there was a lot of focus on this game, with new Leeds coach Garry Monk having started life in West Yorkshire far slower than his counterpart in the opposite dugout. Still under the ownership of Massimo Cellino, there were strong rumours that failure to beat Huddersfield might invite a premature end to Monk's tenure with Leeds, but that never became reality. A tense affair, both teams lacked any real quality in the final third, but Town used the ball far better, and looked much more likely to make an opening. While the early work Town had done in the summer clearly helped them start as quickly as they did, Leeds' similar level of squad turnover seemed nowhere near as effective, and it was a great example of how crucial that work Huddersfield put in away from football with one another really was in the long run.

Having been dull for the majority of the game, with both sides cancelling one another out, there was a flashpoint towards the end of the first half, when Aaron Mooy made a late lunge across a Leeds player, earning himself a yellow card as he went - but the Leeds bench were clearly of the opinion he deserved stronger punishment than the one he received, loudly protesting the decision. Having been uncertain to play after being involved in two matches for Australia during the international break, David Wagner took the risk to start him, in the face of jet lag and fatigue concerns. Despite neither side actually managing a shot on target in the first half, the competition was engaging enough, with both coaches urging their side to keep the ball on the deck and attempt to play football the right way.

Ten minutes into the second half Huddersfield finally made the breakthrough. The ball broke kindly for Aaron Mooy, who was central to the Leeds goal, and around 25 yards out, if not a touch more. Picking his spot, the Australian drove a fierce strike straight past Rob Green and into the top corner, sprinting away to celebrate in front of the travelling Huddersfield support. A largely understated performer, Mooy lost himself in the moment, sparking a pile-on of Town talent at the foot of the away fans, who were celebrating just as wildly just feet away from them. That win, Huddersfield's fifth in six games with a loss yet to be registered, sent them four points clear at the top of the league, while Leeds were left third from bottom, having won just once in six.

It might have been somewhat different though, had Dean Hoyle not gotten his way in the summer transfer window. Having bought Mooy from their sister club in Australia, those in charge of talent management at Manchester City wanted for him to go out on loan in England, and singled out Huddersfield as an ideal destination. Having been given footage of the player and taken a meeting with him and representatives from City at Eric's in Lindley - one of Huddersfield's most widely celebrated restaurants - Hoyle was sure Mooy had to join. David Wagner, it turns out, wasn't.

"We interviewed Aaron Mooy at Eric's one afternoon," starts Hoyle, tapping on the table in front of him. "There was me, Brian Marwood from Manchester City, Aaron and David Wagner. David tells me, you can't sign Aaron Mooy because I've never seen him play. I was gobsmacked. I kept saying to David and Stuart Webber, he's fantastic, we've got to sign him. I kept asking Stuart Webber, what's he saying? I was adamant, we needed to sign Aaron Mooy! Eventually, we bullied him into it and, within two weeks of him arriving, David said, fantastic, thank you. It doesn't always work like that, obviously.

David is very clear, he has to see players in the flesh first, which I completely understand. It's funny how football works, but there was just something in me that said he was a player we had to have at Town."

Taking that story back to David Wagner, he laughs as he realises what his boss has let slip. Aaron Mooy would go on to be the standout player in the Championship that season, and central to everything Huddersfield would achieve. Wagner shakes his head as he gives his side of the story.

"This is correct. I don't like to sign players which I've never seen live and as everyone knows, Australia is very far away so I wasn't able to seen Aaron live! Even if I've seen a lot of video footage which impressed me, I still thought, it's a long way from Australia to England, and I was aware he plays for the Australia national team. I was well aware of all the travelling he would have to do in the international breaks, because I've done it as a player in the other direction to America from Germany - it's not easy. I know how hard that was and how tired you can feel after those international breaks, and that's really what I had in my head when I was saying no.

"After I spoke with Dean and found out that Aaron had been in England previously and played in the youth academy at Bolton before moving to Scotland, I felt better. His wife is even Scottish, too. There were some other things that were persuading me so I thought, come on, this is something we should try. So yes, it's correct that Dean played a part in the conversations we had, and if I had my way first, I didn't think it made much sense bringing this Australian guy across to come and play in the Championship. Of course, I can say now that it was a very good move, and I am happy that it happened."

Sadly, that run for Town came to an end in disappointing fashion away to Brighton, with what should have finished 0-0 becoming a 1-0 Brighton win, after young Town goalkeeper Danny Ward allowed a tame Anthony Knockaert strike to ghost through him in the final stages, leaving Town just ten minutes to try and rescue something from the game. Both teams registered the same three shots on target and narrowly split the possession 51% in favour of Huddersfield, so without the mistake, it's clear a scoreless draw would've been the fairest result. A harsh way for Town to lose their first game of the season, and something 23-year-old Ward will certainly have learnt from and used as a stepping stone in his own progression, it's still somewhat encouraging that away against one of the sides who've spent the most time at the top of the Championship in recent history, Huddersfield more than held their own for the majority.

Returning to the sanctity of home where they were still yet to drop points, Huddersfield notched up yet another 2-1 win, with Kasey Palmer and Elias Kachunga scoring in either half. Both goals came from headers, with Rajiv van La Parra assisting the first, and Tommy Smith the second, getting forward from right-back and making his delivery count. There was a late headed goal from Idrissa Sylla, too, which made things far tighter than they ever ought to have been, but in the post-game press conference, David Wagner claimed he didn't have the vocabulary to express how happy he was, clearly proud his side managed to dust themselves off after their first defeat of the season and remain two points clear at the top of the table.

Losing their second away game on the run, Huddersfield only had individual mistakes and themselves to blame yet again. For some reason, having been awarded a free kick of his own, Rajiv van La Parra decided to talk back to referee James Linington earning his second yellow, getting himself sent off in under half an hour for dissent. In the end, Reading did need a wicked deflection to get through Town's excellent defence, but it was clear to most how and why Town struggled in the game, with David Wagner coming to the defence of his player when faced with the press. While he was quick to acknowledge a mistake was made and conversations would be had internally, no blame was attributed for the defeat. Finishing the game strongly, Huddersfield could've easily taken something from the game on another day, but on this occasion, karma seemed determined to keep Reading in front.

Like clockwork, back in the John Smith's Stadium for their next game, Town were back to winning ways. Their sixth straight home win of the season, Kachunga had his side in front within two minutes, making an intelligent run behind the Rotherham line after sustained Huddersfield pressure, forcing the ball past a helpless goalkeeper. When the Rotherham equaliser did come, it was against the run of play, and their only shot on target within the whole game. Within five minutes of former Terrier Danny Ward volleying past then Town loan goalkeeper Danny Ward (what do you know? it's a fairly common name) Nahki Wells had Town back ahead, with neither side coming all that close to doing anything in the second half, although Huddersfield did have the possession needed to make something happen if needed. The win took them back to the top of the Championship, two points clear of second place.

A constant in these early games, and a theme behind many of their victories, is how much better settled and organised Huddersfield looked playing against the majority of sides they faced, with players never unsure of where their next pass was coming from, or looking short or without support in any areas. The key behind that, David Wagner's 4-2-3-1 formation, was something he brought in from day one, and was clearly the system he thought best for both the players he had at his disposal and the league he was having to compete in. With many sides playing in a far flatter 4-4-2, or a rather more defensive 5-3-2, the shape Town held gave them the best of both worlds - the ability to be both robust without the ball, but deadly effective with it. Speaking to Wagner about it, the use of that system appeared to be more about familiarity and, having watched footage of the team extensively before joining, identifying that this could be a system to take them to the next level.

"In the end it's very easy, so even if I'm totally adaptable to everything, I'm used to this system and I can see a lot of advantages in this system, even if I know disadvantages or advantages of other formations as well. I've seen a lot of games on video of the team before I joined and I thought, they have the players to play this formation and if I'm used to this formation and trust it and have the players to play it, then why not? In the interviews, I explained why this would be the case, my ideas, what I wanted to bring up with the individual players and how that might make the team better. During that process I think they realised, okay, this could work out. This was why I said, ok, this is the right set up, the right formation for these types of players, and it's correct for the players I've brought here in the summer, too. It was never a question about two strikers or a three at the back - it was just that, at the time when we arrived, we had exactly the players we needed to play this formation, and to play it well."

It's fascinating to talk tactics and the minutiae of the game with a coach like David, because he's clearly spent so much time studying and pondering these types of questions already, trying to make himself the best possible coach he can be. His office is a giveaway into how he operates, too. There are dual doors that open into the space his assistants share, which are only closed occasionally for privacy. Everything has a place, there's no mess, and all of the surfaces are empty unless there's a function for what is on it. There's no frills, nothing flashy, just a tablet at one side of his desk and a laptop on the other. His bookshelf includes a title on Bill Shankly, nodding to the history of the club, and at the end of it is tied a blue and white scarf, which is very much a symbol of the present. There's a whiteboard on the largest wall, with the entire season plotted out ahead of him, with fixtures and training noted down, plans already in place months in advance of when they'd be needed. David Wagner clearly isn't a man that does things by accident, and how the team play is a reflection of that.

Having recruited especially to play in that shape, the reason Wagner preaches fitness so much is because that is what his system requires to function. His full-backs have to be able to fly back and forth the entire game, being defensively sound, but providing natural width when Town's inverted wingers inevitably begin to drift inside. His first band of midfield, made up of a more defensive-minded player and a creative partner - usually Jonathan Hogg and Aaron Mooy - are the hub of the side, doing the lion's share of possession retrieval, with Mooy pivotal in how they play between the opposition's lines, and link their own defensive and attacking departments.

Clearly something he'd brought over with him from Dortmund, it's not exactly the same type of football they play, but his own interpretation and version of that game plan. More possession-based than how his former club are known for playing, and less reliant on having a single main source for goals, Wagner managed to find a way to allow all of his main players flourish under the same shared idea, which is far, far easier said than done. It's infinitely impressive just how quickly Wagner was able to get these nuanced ideas and principles across, and the Town players deserve huge credit for taking them on board in such a short space of time, too.

With a manager less sure of his methods and players unwilling to carry out his every instruction whether results are good or bad, there's no way Huddersfield Town would've been top of the Championship after ten games, and there definitely would've been no reason to think they might have the ability to stay there.

CHAPTER FOUR:

ON OUR WAY?

For the first time in two away games, Huddersfield were able to get a result on their travels, with a 1-0 win at Portman Road the perfect response to their previous narrow losses. A performance without the sort of daft mistakes that cost them against Brighton and Reading, the home side didn't ever really look like troubling Town, with their winner eventually coming from the head of Christopher Schindler after a set play - usually the sort of goal Huddersfield would concede, not score. As usual, it was Town who had more of the ball, but Ipswich were quick and direct enough to ask some questions of the Town defence when going long, but Mark Hudson and Christopher Schindler dealt with that admirably, not allowing Leon Best to use his physicality to disrupt their shape. A win that kept them top of the table, Huddersfield were now playing so well it was prompting unwelcome attention, with David Wagner's name suddenly being linked to every vacant position in England and Germany whenever a coach came to losing their job elsewhere.

Soon came the first of two formal approaches made for Wagner during that period, with Aston Villa having sacked Roberto Di Matteo on the 3rd of October, around four months after they'd hired him in the first place. The odds on Wagner moving to the Midlands began to shoot down at such a rate that, by the end of the week, Huddersfield made the proactive decision to release a statement from Dean Hoyle on the club website, reiterating just how committed both the club and David were to one another, explicitly stating that Wagner would never leave Huddersfield for any of their Championship rivals.

Hoyle told Town's official website: "The club doesn't want to get into a situation where it has to comment every time David or a player is linked with a move away, but setting the position out once will help to set our fans' minds at ease. Like everyone, I know David has aspirations to manage at the highest level – but I also know he wants that to be with Huddersfield, which we're all working to make possible in the future. David has told me that he would never leave us for another Championship club, regardless of which club that is."

An emphatic response to what was at the time quite a scary period for the fan base, who weren't quite sure how much truth there was on the back pages and in the gossip columns. Speaking to them now, neither Hoyle or Wagner is shy about admitting that an offer from Villa was made during that week - but neither seems to treat it with any sort of significance. At the time, most outside the club assumed there was no competition between managing a club with the history, stature and resources of Aston Villa and staying on at Huddersfield, where most still believed the bubble would eventually burst. This was just one of many examples where both Huddersfield Town and David Wagner showed that their relationship was somewhat more than the average club-coach bond, and that mutual desire to succeed with one another became a real theme for the season.

Not a subject Wagner enjoys being drawn on, he maintains that, despite it being a good sign regarding the job you're doing when a club comes in for you, it was never a thought of his to leave Huddersfield during that season, because he was so dedicated to finding out how far exactly he could take the club after such a strong and promising start. "To be honest," he says, letting out a brief sigh as he speaks, "I never left any thoughts of that kind in my head, because I only wanted to see what we can get out of this season. I always said as well, I don't like to speak with anyone until the season is over."

"He's got loyalty." That's what Dean Hoyle has to say of his head coach when the issue of him being poached is brought up. "He's showed loyalty, but loyalty can only go so far. I had to improve his contract, but even when I improved his terms, he was still a mile away from what he could have earned elsewhere.

"I think sometimes it was about when I sat down with David, I said to him, look, contracts are fine, big clubs are fine but I believe you can go further by building the right platform here, because we've had such a great start. His stock is incredibly high and, if he'd gone to Villa, who knows? Steve Bruce is a fantastic manager, but he didn't look like he was going to be able to sort that lot out for a while, and they've had to spend big money in the summer to make it happen. It would've been a waste had he gone last season. He's kind of proved that by showing loyalty, that he likes it here. He made the comments in the press, he'd have felt sick abandoning his players. That was really interesting I thought. He likes it here. I think like I've always said, we're a working class town. The heavy metal football of Dortmund is right up our street, that's a huge mining area as well. There's an obvious overlap and kinship. That means a lot to me."

Results, however, did start proving harder to come by after that episode, whether coincidentally or otherwise. On television for the first time that season against Sheffield Wednesday at home, Town didn't create chances in the way they did usually, and a dubious penalty allowed an away side to win at the John Smith's for the first time that season. Scored by Fernando Forestieri in the 68th minute, had that decision not gone their way, the match could've quite easily ended a draw, and that would have been a much more accurate representation of the game. Town dominated the ball, with Wednesday purposefully standoffish, showing Town a level of respect they wouldn't have dreamt of previously. Huddersfield actually tested Keiren Westwood more than Wednesday did Danny Ward, but just couldn't find the quality to beat him on the day.

A midweek game in Preston followed, and to describe the performance as a hangover would be kinder than required. By far the poorest Huddersfield had been all season, they somehow conspired to concede the same goal three times in a 3-1 loss, and in truth, it might've been more. Preston were able to force Town into making daft fouls in dangerous areas around their own penalty area, and by putting in a series of crosses right on the nose of Danny Ward, who didn't deal with them brilliantly, Preston were able to bundle in a carbon copy of the same goal three times, which made for frustrating viewing. Huddersfield were completely lost in terms of marking, and because Preston had clearly unveiled an insecurity, the threat was met with panic, rather than rational thinking - that wasn't how Town had conducted themselves for the rest of the season. It was a cold, bitter night, and with trouble on the M62 getting there, the Town fans that made the effort to make that trip in terrific numbers deserved something better than what they got, but that really is the danger of being a football fan at the end of the day.

There was temporary respite, thanks to a late, late home win against Derby County, who were one of the division's highest spenders. A game in which neither team really gave an inch, Town did create far more than their somewhat stoic opposition, who did look happy to settle for a point as the clock wore on. Not only did Huddersfield have more of the ball - which was no longer a surprise, by this stage - but they did more with it: hitting four more shots on target than their opposition from Derbyshire, and blasting seven more stray strikes in their direction, too. Deep into added time at the end of the second half by the time the winner did come, it was a Kachunga header from a Harry Bunn cross that did the trick, sending the crowd home in a euphoric mood.

That mood, however, wasn't to last long. Travelling to a Fulham side who were looking for just their second win in ten matches, there was a feeling that Huddersfield were a club playing the type of football Fulham were trying to, but just had more momentum behind what they were doing. None of that was evident on the field. Fulham were 3-0 by half-time and, in truth, it could've been more. Despite having struggled to get to grips with what Slavisa Jokanovic had been asking of them until that point, the west London club appeared to save their Eureka moment for the visit of Town, and continued in a similar vein for the rest of the season. David Wagner said that tactically, there was no use for in-depth analysis, because Town made so many uncharacteristic individual mistakes that he as a coach couldn't legislate for them. By the time the game finished 5-0, there was no doubt which side had been better on the day, despite Town not actually having that bad a day going forward - they only had three less shots than Fulham in total, and those were the additional strikes the home team had on target, too.

There was a hope that a defeat of that magnitude would give Town a renewed sense of purpose going forward, sparking a response in the games to come, but the truth of the matter was, things were actually going to be getting worse before they even came close to getting better. November, it's safe to say, did not go the way Huddersfield had imagined it. With three games to play against opposition that, honestly, they should've been favourites against, Town failed to win a match the whole month - the only time that would happen all season.

A real wake up call for all involved, there was a sense that Town were allowing their winning formula to become too formulaic, giving opposition sides a better idea of how to play against them, and get some joy. Perversely, because teams were actually now aware of how good they were, too, when they came to the John Smith's, sides had stopped trying to win, and that seriously closed up the space that Huddersfield had previously been able to exploit. November was the month, in fact, that Town had to learn how to play like the better team, and be treated like one too - that presented a whole different set of hurdles than the ones that had been facing them previously.

The first game of the month at home to Birmingham was a perfect example of this. In the past, a side of that stature, no matter the form they were in, would come to Huddersfield looking for a result. The John Smith's Stadium wasn't somewhere teams had been used to travelling to with any worries about what might happen to them there, but because of the increased gates, the improved atmosphere and the football being played by Wagner's men, there was finally something for away sides to contend with on arrival. For the first time in a long time, a side like Birmingham were coming to Huddersfield trying not to be beaten, which is an entirely different mentality than what they will've been used to.

In that game, Huddersfield had 65% of the ball, had five shots on target to Birmingham's one, and nine corners to their three. It was, for large parts, an elaborate defence vs attack drill you might find on training pitches across the country, the only difference being, these were professional footballers during a competitive fixture - if anybody needed an example of how far Huddersfield had come, it wasn't the table they should have been looking at, but the way their opposition started treating them. Town had to learn how to handle teams actually being scared of them - and that didn't come overnight.

Reacting to that, you imagine, Town went to Cardiff and experimented with a new shape - matching the Bluebirds like for like in a 3-5-2, hoping that their sudden change of tact might catch their opposition cold. It didn't really work, as they found themselves 2-0 down in under twenty minutes, with Cardiff scoring two goals in two minutes to give themselves a bumper start that Huddersfield wouldn't ever manage to fully overcome. Town did manage to pull one back fairly quickly through Tommy Smith, but Cardiff reinstated their two goal cushion before Town could even threaten an equaliser. Having reverted back to their usual shape midway through the second half and introduced Philip Billing from the bench as an additional attacking threat with the ball, the young Dane would go on to score Town's goal of the season, regardless of it being in consolation.

With an attack breaking down in the box, a loose header away is given by a Cardiff player, with the ball landing centrally, just beyond the 'D' of their penalty area. Taking a few strides towards the ball before swinging his boot through it on the half volley, there is a loud cry of "shoot!" from the Town support in the away end. Obliging, the first time hit from Billing erupts from his foot at the rate of a bullet, and whips itself into the top corner of the goal, giving the keeper no chance to save it whatsoever. In truth, for health and safety reasons, it's probably better off that Ben Amos in the Cardiff goal didn't get a hand to it, because it was travelling at the sort of velocity that would likely damage even the strongest of wrists.

Town did have twenty minutes left to try and find an equaliser, but didn't muster another shot on target. In an odd quirk of the game, in fact, every shot that was on target in this game did result in a goal - Cardiff registered three, and Huddersfield two, which is how the game eventually finished. In isolation, that sort of a mad end-to-end game that the manager has chosen to experiment in isn't actually that big a deal, because on another day, who's to say the ball doesn't end up flying in for Town more than it does for Cardiff? It's hardly as if there was any tangible reason why that game ended up finishing the way it did, given the manner in which it was played. The trouble is, it wasn't a standalone fixture, and to follow up a drab draw at home with a quite frankly crazy game away didn't exactly give off the impression that Huddersfield were any closer to finding a new way to play now that teams weren't taking points against them for granted.

As if to illustrate the point even more, that match was followed by one of Town's worst results and performances of the season: a 2-1 home loss to Wigan, who were far and away one of the most abysmal sides in the Championship that season. It was, by every measure, a complete and utter smash and grab, and in truth, Wigan deserved the points they got for taking their chances in the face of Huddersfield being wholly unable to finish their own. If there were ways to rationalise the previous two results without losing too much heart, this was the outlier - Huddersfield were genuinely poor, perhaps for the first time at home, and it did test the nerves of those who had heard pundits telling them nothing but how Town would eventually drop down the division once their bubble had burst.

Wigan's first goal came on the 40-minute mark, after Huddersfield had spent the majority of the first half playing around the opposition penalty box, occasionally creating half chances that were inevitably missed. Breaking down the right flank through Yanic Wildschut, who was head and shoulders the most dangerous man on the park that night, Town missed two clear chances to tackle him before his cross came in, which Jonathan Hogg couldn't stretch far enough to properly block. The ball kindly fell to Reece Burke, who stood in the middle of the goal at point blank range, and he had the simple task of just knocking it in, leaving Danny Ward no chance at all to save it.

Huddersfield did manage to equalise shortly into the second half, after a nice ball from Stankovic allowed Nahki Wells the room he needed to turn and get behind the Wigan defence. Squaring the ball across the box, Aaron Mooy was on hand to turn it in just beyond the far post, giving Town fans hope that their side might actually come back and win the game. Ten minutes after that goal, however, Huddersfield overcommitted coming forwards, lost the ball midway inside their own half, and left their backline completely exposed, playing a high line and almost sat on halfway. A simple clip of the ball over the top is all it took, with Wildschut already chasing and Town's defence stationary, and the Dutch striker was clean through. Too quick to be caught, he had the presence of mind to clip the ball around the onrushing Danny Ward before applying the finish into an empty goal, which was nothing less than he deserved for his individual performance on the day.

Some fans did complain about the result, and pointed to several entirely feasible penalty decisions that went against them as being the reason for their defeat, but in truth, that's not really the standard Huddersfield were aiming for. Warren Joyce's first win as Wigan manager during the short time he was in charge there, David Wagner chose to ignore the refereeing performance in his post-match reflections too, instead making sure he gave credit to Wigan for coming to play his side with a game plan and executing it perfectly. With the busiest period in the calendar around the corner, Huddersfield had twice as many games scheduled for December as they did in November, with six games to play before the turn of the year. How they fared in that period would ultimately decide just how serious they were as contenders, because in light of the defeat to Wigan and the poor run of results preceding it, Town had fallen out of the top six for the first time all season.

CHAPTER FIVE:

TERRIER SPIRIT

With questions now being asked of Town's quality after a sub-par November, there was a real need to go into December and start quickly - winning, as they say, is a habit, and the longer Huddersfield went without a positive result, the more chance there would be of them falling too far away from the rest of the pack.

Away at Ewood Park in their first game of a month that would see them play six times in total, Blackburn looked like the sort of struggling outfit that Town may be able to take advantage of. With the spirit still high among the Terrier fans, tickets had sold well for the game, with a large number of away supporters making themselves heard at one end of the ground. Blackburn, in the midst of years-long civil war with their ownership, didn't have the crowd they used to, and certainly couldn't boast that type of intimidating atmosphere that might kick their side on. Far from a stick to beat them with, that's more a damning indictment of how poorly run their football club has been, and how much of an adverse effect that can have on a fan base.

Touching on a theme that repeatedly came up when in conversation with Dean Hoyle - honesty - it's interesting to see how his outlook on ownership and leadership clearly differs with what can go on at a club who've been as hard done by as Blackburn, because it helps underline what exactly it is about Hoyle that resonates with Huddersfield fans so fully. While the man himself thinks he's given more rope than most because fans see him as one of their own, he doesn't shy away from sharing the mistakes he's made in the past, that have made him into the figure he is today.

"I think I've always been very honest and straight with Huddersfield fans," he says, clearly searching for an example as he speaks. "It goes back to when I first came into the club, I always knew I wanted to tell the truth - whether fans would like what they heard or not. The first mistake I ever did was when I came into the club, Stan Ternent got appointed as manager by Andrew Watson, who was the chief executive back then. In the board meeting, I got overruled, although I was chairman elect. Ken Davy overruled me, but it was his right to, as he had majority shareholding.

"Despite that, I spoke to the local press at The Examiner and I said, yeah, Stan is the right coach for this club. I looked at the paper after and I thought, what have I said? Why have I said that?! I remember from that point on I thought, okay, I won't be bothered any more. The fans will hear the good, the bad and the ugly whether they want to hear it or not. I think that's probably put me in good stead even more through the difficult times than the good times, because in the good times you don't have to convince anyone. It's in difficult times you've got to really show your mettle and I think if you tell the truth then, even if fans don't want to hear it, but if you tell them it regardless, at least they know exactly how it is."

It's something that David Threlfall-Sykes picked up on, too. Having been at the club long enough to have experienced it under previous ownership, the significance of what changed when Hoyle took charge wasn't ever lost on him, and it remains something he clearly doesn't take for granted.

"We all have a mantra internally," Threlfall-Sykes tells me, "and that comes from Dean: try and be as good as you possibly can in what you do and put the football to one side when doing so.

"In truth, that's hard. Like I say, I started here when it was under previous ownership and without going back over all the history of the feeling at that time, the fan base wasn't overly receptive to what the club had to say at that point, because of the backdrop of the off-field difficulties occurring at the time. Dean gave us an amazing opportunity to put a broom through the place and start again. When he came in as Chairman, we knew we were onto a winner straight away. We've got pictures of Dean in the stands at games from before he took over, and he's got a wig on and all that kind of stuff. We knew him and he was genuine, he had the finances to back up what he wanted to do. He was absolutely perfect - he's like the Carlsberg of Chairmen, if you will.

"At that point, there was such an ill feel around the club that it gave us the opportunity to press the reset button. What I mean by that is, we could start afresh and part of that, we did all this Yorkshire club rebranding - which wasn't to everybody's taste - but the idea behind the process was that we wanted to find an identity again. You end up getting personally tied into your club and you really care about what it stands for as a fan.

"The idea behind the Yorkshire club name was to resonate with our fans - so people who follow Huddersfield Town, what do they love? You know what people from Yorkshire are like, there's a pride in being from here that I don't find in any other county for whatever reason, and all the values that Yorkshire men and Yorkshire women like to think they stand for: like honesty, integrity, straight-talking, all that kind of stuff, it kind of embodied what we wanted to be like as a club, so we brought that in as our brand. Dean was always the face of that, and it'd been an incredibly hard sell without a man like him leading it.

"That first summer when Dean was in charge, I remember we were all at Southend and it felt exciting and it felt new, and there were a lot of things we were doing off the field – like the partnership with Yorkshire Air Ambulance - that contributed to it that summer. It brought pride back to the club, you were proud to be a Huddersfield Town fan and not just because we made a real fist of it in the football sense that season. It felt different, so it allowed us to re-energise the club and attitude surrounding us but, without Dean, I don't think we could have done any of that."

All that said, however, none of it seemed to help when that game at Ewood Park came around. Although there was an immediate response from the Town players, with Kasey Palmer opening the scoring in under ten minutes, they ended the half level, after Blackburn were awarded a penalty ten minutes before half-time. What turned out to be their only on-target strike of the day, Huddersfield would go on to dominate the remainder of the game, but couldn't find the requisite amount of quality needed to make a difference in the final third. So frustrating to watch, the team would win back possession of the ball, with ease, before building a move through midfield, eventually getting the ball to outside the Blackburn box. From there, the result was either one of two things: a strike from range that would either be blocked, be off-target or be so tamely hit that the goalkeeper could save with ease, with the alternative being a nice ball being worked outside, only for the resulting cross to evade everybody it needed to.

That type of performance was becoming a regular

occurrence, sadly, and Huddersfield desperately needed to get themselves out of that repetitive cycle. Five games since their last win - which would go on to be a season-wide record - Town were almost where they needed to be, but not quite. Akin to a car being started that never seems to be able to fully turn over, there was obviously enough there for Huddersfield, but they were lacking the confidence to make it happen.

Next time out, with relegation-threatened Bristol City coming to the John Smith's Stadium, there was another fast Town start, with Elias Kachunga getting Town ahead in just ten minutes, with the energy level on the field far better than it had been. Chelsea youngster Tammy Abraham did equalise in opportunistic fashion just after the half-hour mark, but the crowd at Huddersfield, rather than the players, reacted by taking it up a gear. While the gates had improved at the ground, it was a stadium still finding its voice, but in adversity, they seemed to find a decibel level that they hadn't previously, with over 18,000 in attendance for a game that almost half of them wouldn't have been interested by in any other circumstance.

That change off the field appeared to have the desired

effect on it, with Town taking just over ten minutes of the second half to get themselves back in front. A mistake by the Bristol keeper, one heavy touch in the area was all the invitation Nahki Wells needed to nip in and smash the ball in a virtually open net. While it was far from vintage stuff, it was exactly the kind of break that Huddersfield needed, especially with the form book starting to look as desperate as it was. Three days later, away to Burton Albion, that lift seemed to have a second wind. Heading for a disappointing 0-0 draw, Huddersfield turned the screw in the final ten minutes, and Wells managed to get his head to the winner with only five minutes of normal time remaining.

While it's true that, on paper at least, beating Bristol at home and Burton away is far from the most impressive feat in the world, those victories took Huddersfield back into the top six, which was fast becoming a worry. Having re-established their platform and renewed confidence in themselves, Town wouldn't drop out again for the rest of the season.

Live on Sky again for their next game away at Carrow Road to face Norwich City, this was the perfect opportunity for Huddersfield to not only cement their top six ambitions, but push toward the automatic places, which were still well within touching distance. Having started the season so brightly and held top spot for so long, it was clearly something the players were trying to recapture. 'No limits' was the philosophy, and that's the ideology that they were taking after.

Another quick start, Elias Kachunga fired Town ahead after just five minutes. On the break, Kasey Palmer carried the ball direct towards the box in a central position, before disguising a ball wide to Tommy Smith - who was overlapping in yards of free space - as a shot, giving his full-back and captain all the time he needed to pick out his man. Side-footing a cross straight across the six-yard box at pace, Kachunga was unmarked in the middle, and just needed to make contact to score into an all but empty goal. Within a minute, however, Norwich had levelled, with a poor Robbie Brady cross looping into the area finding the head of Jonny Howson, who managed to do just about enough to guide the ball into the corner.

Just before half-time, though, Huddersfield went on yet another break in what was proving to be a fairly open and attacking game. Elias Kachunga was making a strong run forward, and used Tommy Smith outside him to open up some more space for himself in the middle. Playing what was in truth a fairly basic one-two, that was enough to open Norwich up, giving Kachunga time to skip into the box and get off a strike, which snuck under the body of an extremely slow to react John Ruddy, who must've been unsighted by his defenders. The home side did have the better chances from then on, and probably should've equalised with one of them, but Town managed to hold on for an impressive win, taking themselves out of that November tail spin with three solid victories on the bounce.

This form wasn't going unnoticed, however, and for the second time that season, a formal approach was made to take David Wagner away from Huddersfield, with Wolfsburg having tabled an offer. The reports in the German press did make the appointment sound like a forgone conclusion, and far more than the Aston Villa query, there was a real worry that a club of such significant size in the Bundesliga might be enough to prize the manager away. As is club policy, Town decided to stay quiet on the matter for as long as they could, but while stories continued in both Germany and England, the coach was given little choice but to address what was going on, and did so via another club statement.

"There have been a lot of rumours around my future in the media, and although I don't believe I should be the story, I cannot stay silent on this matter," David Wagner would express in a club statement. "It is correct that there has been interest from a few Bundesliga clubs. They have obviously seen the way we are going at Huddersfield Town and the journey we have been on together over the last 12 months. It's important for me to clarify that my focus is on moving forward at Huddersfield Town. We want to develop what has been a good season so far into a great one, with the staff, players and fans together as one. I ask our fans to keep up the superb support they have given the players all season, starting with the game against Nottingham Forest on Boxing Day. We are creating something special here."

While it's one thing to say no to another club in your division, to turn down a job of that magnitude in your homeland is another thing altogether. You wouldn't ever imagine an English coach going to manage abroad in the German second flight at a smaller club being offered the Everton job, for example, and turning it down, would you?

It was an amazing show of loyalty and faith, yet again, and the type of renewed commitment that gave Huddersfield and its fan a skip back in their step.

Given the tone of the reports, however, Dean Hoyle went out of his way to remind everyone just who Huddersfield Town are, putting up a fight for the honour of his club, and setting a few misconceptions straight as he did so. "Huddersfield Town may not be a Bundesliga club or one that plays in European competition, but make no mistake - we are a serious, proud, ambitious club with a rich history," Hoyle said. "Perhaps this isn't clear to some of our colleagues in the media in Germany considering the tone of some articles that were published over the last 48 hours," he continued.

"We are not to be toyed with or dismissed out of hand. We have values and always conduct ourselves in the right manner; something that cannot be said for other clubs. I think David's ongoing commitment to Huddersfield Town is testament to this club and its standing. He's turned down several advances from Bundesliga clubs during his time here, the latest coming very, very recently. It is important to be clear on this," Hoyle added. "The day will come when David moves on, as is the case with every manager or head coach at every club in world football. However, that day is not upon us."

Having asked, neither David or Dean confirmed who the other Bundesliga clubs alluded to are, but there was some talk that relegation-threatened FC Ingolstadt were interested in his services - but if he wasn't going to Wolfsburg, he certainly wasn't going to be going there, either. It's interesting to speak to Hoyle about this though, because he's fairly clear about knowing that David's ambition and ability are likely to take him away from Huddersfield one day, but for as long as he can, he's going to fight it, and make Town the most attractive place for Wagner to be head coach. One of those techniques - rewarding the coaching staff with several new deals while they've been at the club - is less to do with sentiment, and far more to do with asset management. It's in exchanges like these that you suddenly remember just how much the man opposite you is worth, and how exactly he got there.

"I can assure you," Hoyle says, using a far more serious tone than he had previously, "while it's good for morale to renew a contract, the reasoning behind that is to make sure I secure assets. If you want to look at it through a fairytale lens, you might think I'm just being a kind chairman that's doing right by people - but the people who've got contracts, including the coach, have got contracts because I want to secure in that position and to this club. There's nothing more romantic to it than that, really. I've realised we're onto something and that David is brilliant at what he does, so it's as simple as that."

Speaking to David about it, he sounded far less bothered about what he would be joining, and more concerned with what he would be leaving behind. To leave Huddersfield at that time would've left him with a significant 'what if' hanging over his head, and that doesn't sound like something he was interested in going through. "In the period around Christmas, everyone knows the rumours about the options I had to coach elsewhere, but I decided to stay here in this football club. Around that time at Christmas I really thought we can come into the top six, and we would have a chance. If you're in the top six, everything is possible. I thought about it, and knew I would like to experience the full season, and see what is really achievable. I don't think I'd ever wanted to leave not knowing what would've happened, especially when I thought that we might have a chance."

Perhaps with that having provided a distraction away from their training and meticulous preparation, Town started slowly on Boxing Day, and Nottingham Forest took the lead after just 25 minutes, capitalising on a fairly flat performance from the home side. A quirk of their results, Town hadn't actually won a game all season in which they'd fallen behind at this point, which did leave some in the crowd aware of the stat far more nervous than they needed to be. After the interval, Huddersfield came out much more like themselves, and forced the tide of the game to change, with Forest staging their own meltdown greatly helping matters, as well. Equalising after less than ten minutes into the second period through Kasey Palmer, there was only five minutes between that going in and the eventual winner, with Michael Mancienne putting through his own goal just before the hour mark. The result of the game wasn't really in doubt after that point, with Mancienne later putting a cherry on the top of his particular Christmas cake by getting a second yellow and being sent off in the 89th minute. Suppose that's one way to get a break over the festive period.

It was at this stage that, in the face of the overwhelming evidence in front of them, most people started to allow themselves some thoughts about the play-offs being a possibility, and where that might eventually lead to. Asking the question to various figures across the club - when did you allow yourself to start to imagine? - the same answer came around time and time again. Christmas.

"We all got to the point where we said look, when we've played everyone once, we'll take proper stock of where we are," David Threlfall-Sykes tells me. "I think we played everyone once by Boxing Day, and when we'd got there, we were still comfortably fourth in the table - that's probably when I first thought to myself wow, we've got a chance. We're doing alright. By that point you'd seen what every other team had to offer and you'd not seen anything that scared you, blew you away or was a different level than what we could play. Once we got to Christmas, I think that's when you quietly start to think to yourself, we might be onto a winner here."

Christopher Schindler, who was well on his way to confirming himself as the single best central defender in the Championship by this stage, says he always knew this Town team were good, but even they started to surprise themselves. "When I played the pre-season, I felt like the team was really good," he tells me, sipping on a coffee between training sessions. "We were way better than the team I used to play for from a footballing quality angle, but obviously I didn't know how good the other teams were in the Championship at that stage, and with the winning streak at the beginning of the season wasn't what I was told to expect. I felt like, these are really good results, but obviously every game was close. We won a lot of games where there was only one goal the difference. I think at Christmas time, when we were still up there, we felt if we keep going we had a good chance to reach the play-offs."

It's a sentiment that Tommy Smith echoes, too. One of the most interesting Town players to speak to, in fact, there's a deliberate point behind everything Smith says, and you can see him working out what the best way to phrase an answer is while you talk. Brilliantly articulate and interesting to hear speak, there's no question over why he has the armband after you spend even a short amount of time with him. There's a level of care and pride in everything he does that mirrors his head coach, and you'd imagine that's what had allowed them to have such a mutually beneficial relationship.

"I think we always had it in the back of our minds for some time, to be honest," Smith says of finishing in the top six, and going for promotion. "If you were to ask the players deep down what they felt, early on we could feel something special was happening. I think by Christmas we were really in the mix for it. It's probably after Christmas it became apparent that teams were starting to fear us, even though one or two had already started setting up that way against us. Again, secretly, deep down you have that confidence in your head, thinking that we can keep this up and do it here. When the pundits were having their say and people outside the club having their say, it was like, just ignore them. That's how we've always been. Ignore what people are saying, and focus on yourself. It was about self belief and being able to concentrate on yourselves as part of the football club, and that was the message throughout the whole season."

Unfortunately, however, the month ended very much as it began - with an underwhelming 1-1 draw with Blackburn, this time at home. Rovers would go on to be relegated that season, and you could see why, but for some reason, they appeared impervious to whatever Huddersfield threw at them. Not once, but twice. Terrible to watch the entire game, Blackburn defended with almost everybody they had on the edge of their own box, giving Huddersfield absolutely no space to play in. Just to underline that point, when the game finished, Town had registered 18 separate shots, and Blackburn just the one. Maddeningly, just after the 80th minute, Blackburn pumped a deep free-kick into the box, and managed to collect the second ball as it broke down, swinging a cross in from the right. With the Town players still recovering position after the set play, Danny Graham managed to find half a yard he wouldn't have had otherwise, finding the bottom corner with his header.

Town tried their luck more than once after falling behind, but if anything, Blackburn were even deeper than they had been previously, and they really did have every man behind the ball, now. It wasn't until deep into injury time when, luckily, Huddersfield were given a free-kick right on the whitewash of the penalty area, just left of centre. Pulling rank over Aaron Mooy and Jack Payne, Nahki Wells took the kick himself, delicately floating the ball up and over the wall and into the back of the net at a pedestrian pace, having hardly taken a run up. In a game that was severely lacking quality, it was a piece of play that was significantly out of place. Had it come even five minutes sooner, there may have been enough time in the match to fully turn it around, but the referee was looking to blow his whistle for full-time even before that free-kick was taken.

Despite ending 2016 on a somewhat disappointing note, Huddersfield had given themselves a clear platform for the remainder of the season, especially after going undefeated through December, getting four wins from six, beating everyone that wasn't Blackburn. Just over half the season in, Huddersfield found themselves fourth in the Championship going into 2017, having spent eight earlier rounds of the campaign on the summit. This, of course, was only the start.

CHAPTER SIX:

RENEWED COMMITMENT

January was another extremely busy month for Town, with five games to play at quick succession. A little over a year since Wagner had taken over, the club couldn't have been more different than one he joined. By this point, the majority of the infrastructural changes that Wagner desired had been implemented, and the club were pushing themselves to find new ways of improving, too. That's the funny thing about being successful - once you know something is working, you do all you can to maximise that. Having come through a rough period and got themselves back on track, and retained their head coach in the face of numerous attempts to take him elsewhere, 2016 was not a boring time to follow Huddersfield Town, and 2017 was ready to follow suit.

It's a time that Dean Hoyle remembers fondly and, much

David Wagner's first press conference as Huddersfield Town head coach, alongside then chief executive Nigel Clibbens. [John Early]

David Wagner (right) with assistant coach Christoph Buhler (left) during his very first training session at PPG Canalside. [John Early]

Opening day victory against Brentford, with the Town players making their way over to the South Stand to celebrate.

Jack Payne celebrates his late winner away at St James' Park, where Town won 2-1 early in the season. [Robbie Jay Barratt]

Aaron Mooy celebrates his long-range winner against Leeds United away at Elland Road. Town won 1-0, keeping them top of the Championship. [John Early]

Aaron Mooy is under there, somewhere, after scoring his sensational winner at Elland Road.

Michael Hefele celebrates scoring one of two goals away to Rochdale in the FA Cup, which Town won 4-0.

Walking to the ground ahead of the West Yorkshire derby against Leeds United.

Cult hero Michael Hefele celebrates his last-minute winner against Leeds United as only he can – with trademark claws. [John Early]

Town captain Tommy Smith looks unsure what to do with himself, having just scored the winner in his side's 3-2 victory away at Rotherham with virtually the last kick of the game. [John Early]

Huddersfield Town 0-0 Manchester City in the FA Cup, securing a fifth-round replay.

A taste of what was to come, in an FA Cup replay at the Etihad, against Pep Guardiola's Manchester City.

Huddersfield Town 3-0 Norwich City, under a beautiful Yorkshire sunset.

The John Smith's Stadium at near capacity in the sunshine, awaiting kick-off in the first leg of the semi-final play-off against Sheffield Wednesday.

Danny Ward saves Fernando Forestieri's penalty to win the shootout and book Huddersfield's place at Wembley in the play-off final. [John Early]

Arm-in-arm, the players show their appreciation to the Huddersfield fans, a familiar sight throughout the season. [John Early]

Chairman Dean Hoyle leads his players in their celebrations at Hillsborough.
[John Early]

Central defenders Michael Hefele and Christopher Schindler give a joint interview at the play-off final press day at PPG Canalside.

Town manager, David Wagner, on media duty at PPG Canalside on play-off final press day.

Town captain Tommy Smith answering questions during the play-off final press day.

Fans take the famous walk along Wembley Way ahead of the play-off final, with the national stadium's arch in the background.

Reading FC vs Huddersfield Town, 2016–17 Championship play-off final, Wembley Stadium.

The biggest kick in Huddersfield Town's modern history. He didn't miss.
[John Early]

Christopher Schindler skips away, having just scored the decisive penalty at Wembley, securing promotion. [John Early]

UNDERDOG

The dream comes true.

Mark Hudson lifts the play-off trophy with his team at Wembley, helping to get celebrations underway. [John Early]

Premier League status confirmed, Mark Hudson and Tommy Smith share the honours. [John Early]

David Wagner with the play-off trophy at Wembley, dressed for the occasion. [John Early]

Huddersfield players dance at Wembley, celebrating with fans.

An elated David Wagner on the customary open-top bus parade, as it makes its way through the fan-filled streets of Huddersfield. [John Early]

Statue of former prime minister, Harold Wilson, showing off his true colours in St George's Square, Huddersfield.

The climax of the celebration parade in St George's Square, Huddersfield.
[John Early]

the same as everyone else, was the stage in the season where he began to let his mind wander. "Coming through that Christmas period the way we did was huge," he says, still looking somewhat relieved, even just thinking back on it. "We had a bit of a dip, but we came back, and then I actually looked at us and thought - we look really good. It was probably that time when I thought, yeah, we've got a real chance here. I gave David a new contract around then too, which meant he got two new contracts out of me last year, but it was deserved. I knew the common denominator here was the coach to be fair. I don't think there's any denying that."

With the fixture congestion at its worst in the period going from December into the New Year, and the domestic schedule being as tough as it is for Championship clubs already with so many matches to play - especially with the FA Cup getting into full swing at the same time - it was interesting to get Wagner's perspective on how that affected the football being played. Coming from Germany and still relatively inexperienced as a head coach of a senior side, how did the culture of English football surprise him, if at all? Is the Championship just a league full of low-skilled players hoofing long balls, trying to kick and head their way to victory?

"I would say this is partly correct," he says, thinking about how best to elaborate. "I think as more and more foreign managers come into the Championship, the greater the variety of styles you have to play against there become. That's a good thing for the quality of the football and the fans, I think. Yes, it's more direct and maybe a bit more physical, but I think the biggest difference is the amount of games you have to play. Maybe too many, to be honest, especially when there are cup games starting as well.

"You have less time to train and prepare for matches as you would wish as a result, and you have to have a big squad to cope with that, which costs a lot of money, which some clubs don't have at this level. For me, I know I tried to keep the best balance I could between recovery time and training properly, because you have to have as much of the squad as fit, rested and healthy for each coming game, otherwise you will have no options or consistency. That's one of the biggest differences between the Championship and what we have in Germany, or even in the Premier League, to be honest, aside from the quality of the individuals. Every single

Premier League team is better than 21 or 22 of the Championship teams, no doubt."

There is a clear reluctance in Wagner to speak out of turn where English football is concerned, because there are several points at which he stops saying something and starts saying something else in a far more complimentary manner, which is an admirable quality. He's never not aware of how his words may be perceived, but manages to keep the platitudes to a minimum regardless. You still get the truth from Wagner, but you get a slightly diluted version if you stumble over a contentious topic. It's an infectious quality though, but that appears to just be his natural personality - warm, outgoing, humorous and thoughtful. It makes a nice change from the type of coaches who treat their time having to speak about football and their work as a chore, whereas Wagner never makes a question or interview feel like an imposition. By extension, those are exactly the type of qualities that make him popular with not only the fans and staff at Huddersfield, but his players, too. He's the type of man you can see yourself trying your best for, because he would always appear to be doing the same for you.

"You get somewhat of a feeling for him as a person via his various media commitments, because he is what he is on camera, there's no persona," David Threlfall-Sykes believes. Working with the coach closely behind the scenes and in front of the press, he's perhaps the person who's best placed to evaluate just how genuine he appears to be. "It's important to say that because David's got quite a big personality, but it isn't something he puts on for the camera. He's not different behind the scenes - he's a genuine person, he's a really infectious person to be around. He was actually asked recently about how he was finding life in Yorkshire, and he started talking about the people here, saying they're very similar to Germans - in that they're very direct. Then he joked that it was maybe sometimes too direct...

"He likes that about working here, I think. People won't sugar-coat things but they're honest, they work hard, they enjoy what they do - it's all the things that David is in himself as well. It's remarkable how many values of the club and the town he already had before he arrived, because I think, football aside, that's why he was such a great fit straight away. As much as other people haven't been able to get the measure of the place and our fans, David from day one has behaved as if he were tailor-made for Huddersfield Town, which is as important as him being really good as a football manager, to us."

His ability coaching a football team was only becoming more evident, too. Going away to Wigan to start the year, Wagner showed that he was able to adapt and learn from previous mistakes, giving Wigan no opportunity whatsoever to hit Town on the break as they had done earlier in the season. Keeping the game as tight as possible, matching the home team in physicality and only really pumping their foot on the accelerator in the final quarter of the game, Huddersfield effectively used their fitness to their advantage, safe in the knowledge that they would have the fresher legs come the closing stage of the match. There's a confidence needed to perform in that manner, and that had been fostered across the first half of the season already - this was now a side who weren't just able, but comfortable in the knowledge that they were. Nahki Wells scored the winner in the 80th minute, and it came as a result of Huddersfield overloading Wigan in the final third, and them not being able to live with it. Akin to a boxer waiting for their opponent to tire before throwing the knockout punches in the twelfth round, it was a game that said Town weren't just becoming a better team, but a smarter one, too.

That game was followed by an FA Cup third round tie at home to Port Vale, in which a heavily rotated Town side eased their way to a 4-0 win. Allowing for rotation players to show their ability, it also marked the debut of Izzy Brown in a Huddersfield shirt, having been signed on loan until the end of the season the day before from Chelsea, who had recalled him from Rotherham in order to find him a more suitable team to play for. Having been head and shoulders above for the South Yorkshire club, the decision was made by Michael Emenalo - technical director at Chelsea - to relocate one of the club's most promising young players, and Huddersfield fit the bill, with Kasey Palmer having already come on leaps and bounds under David Wagner's wing.

A slower game than usual, with the gulf in class between the two sides evident from the off, it took Huddersfield the best part of half an hour to break through, with Jack Payne finishing off a Joe Lolley assist. Port Vale proved stubborn, and it wasn't until late in the second half when their fitness abandoned them that Huddersfield were really able to pad out the scoreline. First, there was a finish from range by Kasey Palmer, which was closely followed by a Harry Bunn strike from close range and a second for Jack Payne, who was a standout on the day. It was a great example of how Wagner managed to get the most out of his squad, even when not playing regularly. By making training such a dynamic activity and giving each player the same level of preparation, fitness work and appreciation of the tactical nuances of their role, he was able to stretch the depth of his squad more than other coaches may have been able to.

With games coming faster than they'd have probably liked, their next trip was to Hillsborough, in a repeat of Wagner's very first game in charge. Wednesday were going well at the time, chasing the top six and trying to get themselves in a good position to secure a play-off berth, and a win against Town would've greatly helped their chances. With almost 30,000 at the ground to watch the cross Yorkshire derby, the first half proved uneventful, with Wagner and Carlos Carvalhal - the Wednesday coach - cancelling each other out, neither wishing to be caught overexposed or overcommitting in attack. This was a repeat of the pattern that took up much of the first encounter of the season, too, and it was only a penalty on that day that operated the two. After an equally curious start to the second half, the game looked to be heading for a draw when, ten minutes into the second half, Ross Wallace picked up the ball unmarked in the centre of the field and unleashed an unstoppable drive from almost fully thirty yards, giving Danny Ward no chance whatsoever to save it. Huddersfield did then have to open themselves up more in search of an equaliser, and a red card for Jack Payne on the stroke of 70 minutes didn't help matters, either. In added time at the end of the game, with Town a man light and still chasing a point, Wednesday made the scoreline look far more comfortable than it actually was, with Fernando Forestieri adding an extremely late second.

Given the relative size and expenditure of the two sides, it just goes to show how well recruited and trained Huddersfield were, to live with a side like Sheffield Wednesday, and give them two games where they were only narrowly able to sneak a win. Even at Hillsborough, it was Huddersfield who tested the Wednesday defence more, and got better openings and opportunities to strike on goal, but they just didn't have the quality required to make that breakthrough, which was a frustrating tangent that existed right the way across the season. Neither were confident displays, and they weren't the type of matches where you'd be able to pick who was clearly the better side, so that's a massive positive for Town, and a really encouraging nugget to hold onto going into the business half of the season.

Brushing themselves off in preparation for Ipswich to visit, Town knew from the first game at Portman Road that Mick McCarthy was going to keep his team extremely tight, and try and frustrate his way to a result. Opposing ideologies between Wagner and McCarthy, this game is a great example of how Huddersfield appointing a manager from the left field stood them apart from the usual standard in the Championship, with McCarthy part of the furniture at that level. Ipswich may have had a small budget and over performed from time to time, but there wasn't an excitement about them like there was at Huddersfield, and that's because their manager prioritised pragmatism over entertainment, while David Wagner never has. Huddersfield had spent years dealing with coaches of that same ilk, but it had gotten them nowhere - the same could be said for Ipswich, too.

The game was, in truth, a fairly basic non-event. Huddersfield were much the better team from the first kick, and Ipswich didn't have the quality or tactical intelligence to live with them. In lieu of that, they fouled their way to five yellow cards, all given in the second half. It did take Huddersfield some time to break through, with Izzy Brown scoring his first goal for the club just before half-time, but it always felt like a matter of when, rather than if. Christopher Schindler got in on the act shortly after the break, converting a loose ball after a set play, and there was never any danger of Ipswich doing anything to harm Huddersfield at the other end of the field. It was a true case of a better team with a more sophisticated approach to the game keeping the more basic side at arm's length, and doing just about enough to get past them without having to push into their highest gear.

This would become a recurring theme - Huddersfield looking fitter, better prepared and more switched on to what was happening around them. Not only were they the better team physically and technically, but they were making a better collective mental state count, too. More than most, kitman Andy Brook gets to see the team interact with one another while nobody else is watching, and it's in those candid moments that you might be able to see if there are cliques within the squad, or if their enthusiasm on the field wasn't matched off it. According to Brooky, though, it was more their spirit and togetherness being more than what people saw that propelled them along than anything else.

"I say it all the time," he says, "I don't think their success was down to just football. It was the togetherness of the camp, and the way the lads were with each other every day. The changing room was a pleasure to be in, because they'd all be talking, smiling and joking, always together, never in small groups. On days where they can afford to, they come in and have a bit of fun with each other, taking that time to be a little bit less serious. When work needed to be done though, it was done properly, and the atmosphere in the camp never suffered because of that.

"They probably spend longer training than any other club in the country, and they're not complaining about it the way you'd think a footballer would," Brooky says, perhaps speaking more as a fan than an employee. "Little things like that, they seemed to get it right. They're really professional, really good lads but when they realised that, that's when it seemed to come together. Good people, good life, and then it seemed to get a really good team spirit. Honestly, the lads were not like they were at other clubs we visited, and it's not something I've really seen here before, either. They're just normal lads who've got their feet planted on the ground - you could have a chat with them and it's fine, no fuss. Nobody behaving like they're above the staff or the club, which doesn't always happen. Like I say though, the togetherness was unbelievable. I can't speak highly enough of that."

Taking that spirit into the fourth round of the FA Cup, where they'd been drawn away to Rochdale, it was another comfortable 4-0 win against lower league opposition for a much rotated Town side, with a second and final January addition making his debut via the completion, too. Collin Quaner, a striker by trade who can also play on the wing, joined from Union Berlin for an undisclosed fee, with David Wagner looking to add some variety to his forward line. Quaner began the game in centre forward position, and scored the opening goal of the game against the run of play. Due to bad weather, an awful pitch and robust opposition, Town weren't able to play their usual game, with Rochdale threatening more than once through route one balls across the top and strong set plays. Due to a poor kick from their keeper, though, Town were given a two on one in attack late in the second half, and Quaner opened his account for the club with a tap in.

At half-time, David Wagner changed the side completely, bringing on Michael Hefele - the central defender - and playing him up front. Huddersfield then went like-for-like with Rochdale, deciding they could not play on that surface either, and voluntarily took themselves down to that level, because needs must. In what was a bizarre half of football, Hefele managed to score twice, once with his head from a set play, and another as a centre forward would, backing up play on the break and finishing confidently when the ball was squared to him. In the midst of all that, Izzy Brown did score a penalty to make it 2-0, but that was somewhat overshadowed by the Bavarian defender cutting loose and letting his inner goalscorer out, much to the delight of everyone in attendance. Hefele, a cult figure from almost the second he joined Town, has one of the most infectious personalities going, and that immediately resonated. With a mop of long blonde hair and the type of rounded face that belongs more behind a set of drums with a ripped t-shirt than playing professional sport, he was just one of many reasons why that team managed to capture the hearts and imagination of their fan base with so much ease. If not for anything else, that Rochdale game will be remembered as 'that time Hef went up top and scored two'.

With a busy February on the horizon, with six league games to fulfil and big clashes with rivals towards to the top of the league, what Huddersfield maybe could've done without is a distracting FA Cup tie in the fifth round. Naturally, they drew Pep Guardiola's Manchester City at home. No biggie, then.

CHAPTER SEVEN:

WE SHOULDN'T BE LOSING TO TEAMS LIKE HUDDERSFIELD

While it might sound a tad dramatic to give a run of fixtures 'make or break' status with thirteen games still to come after it, February was a bit of a make or break season for Huddersfield Town.

The month would start with the visit of Brighton, who Town were but inches behind in the race for automatic promotion, and be followed up with Leeds United coming to town, in one of the most high-profile West Yorkshire derbies in recent history. Then, there was a trip to London for Huddersfield, with Queens Park Rangers waiting, now managed by one Ian Holloway, which brought its own significance. To round out the month, a home tie in the fifth round of the FA Cup against Manchester City would be sandwiched between two away days in South Yorkshire, with both Rotherham and Barnsley well up for raining on Town's play-off parade. Six big, individually significant fixtures in just 23 days - for a side who'd craved relevance again for so long, this was the type of calendar those fans must've been beside themselves to see.

With over 20,000 packed into the John Smith's Stadium for the Brighton game, this was the game where the atmosphere went from being great, to something genuinely special. Even before a ball had been kicked, the anticipation in the air had the crowd buzzing. It was infectious to be around, and given that the hope was that Town may gatecrash the top two with a positive result, everybody knew what was on the line. Having been to games previously in years gone by with the stadium half empty and most of those in attendance only there through force of habit or masochistic tendencies, this was as clear a signal of how far the club had come under Wagner than anything else. It was an excitement that hadn't just spread amongst fans, but actually punctuated through to the mood of the town - somewhat reminiscent of how everybody pulls together when there's a World Cup or Olympics on, Huddersfield was a town united in hope, and Brighton felt the full force of that.

Starting so quickly that Albion skipper Bruno was booked inside a minute, it took Town less than ten to get in front, with Tommy Smith striking his side into an early lead. Not long after Rajiv van La Parra had given the Brighton upright a warning smack, he picked up the ball in the hole behind the striker, drove across the field and played a strong pass into the right channel, for Smith to gather. Attempting to cross it first time, Smith's ball ricocheted off the feet of the nearest defender and back into his path, leaving him open and in possession in a danger area. Shooting with his left, his strike crept past the keeper at the near post, with a possible deflection helping it on its way. Within ten minutes of that happening though, Aaron Mooy - who rarely but a pass wrong all season - put too much on a head back towards his central defenders, and inadvertently played Tomer Hemed clean through in behind. Rounding an advancing Danny Ward with relative ease, the Israeli international made it 1-1 against the run of play, despite the best efforts of Chris Lowe's to stop the ball crossing the line.

It did take Huddersfield five minutes after being pegged back to regather their momentum, but once they did, Brighton were quickly on the back foot again. Strangely, it was as if Brighton hadn't watched any tapes of Town playing that season, because they just didn't look prepared to be pressed highly up the field, or the pace with which possession would transition from defence to attack, often being left to chase back in numbers before the home side could capitalise on their sudden numerical advantage. Fifteen minutes after the Brighton goal he gave away, Mooy exchanged a neat one-two with Wells down the left channel, before coming inside and playing a beautifully disguised reverse pass through to Elias Kachunga, who was running across the face of the box. Brighton, having bunched around the ball, forgot about Wells - who'd continued his run from earlier - over their shoulder, so when Kachunga was slide-tackled and the ball squired through in the area, the Bermudan was on hand to accept possession. Having the presence of mind to allow the ball to run across his body, Wells then hit it back across the keeper with his right boot, rifling the ball into the opposite top corner. One of the most aesthetically pleasing finishes of the season, it was all about just how cleverly the front four of Huddersfield were able to use their movement, which had become a hallmark of their attack.

On the stroke of half-time, it was Aaron Mooy again who played the killer ball, supplying the pre-assist (if you will) for a third and final Town goal. Picking up a loose ball that had popped out of a duel just ahead of him, Mooy span and carried the ball into space, with Izzy Brown giving him an option down the right, and Wells in space further out on the left. Noticing that Brown had just strayed off side, the Australian international adjusted his foot as he was about to play his pass, and zipped it wide to Wells, who had the already cautioned Bruno to beat one-on-one. Deciding to allow the ball wide onto his left rather than exchange the defender next to him, Wells hit a hard strike back across David Stockdale in the Albion goal, forcing him to parry the ball back out into danger. Following in from the opposite wing, Elias Kachunga had the easiest header in the world to give his side some breathing room going into half-time, and didn't make a mistake. After the break, little of note happened, but Huddersfield were still playing at a high enough tempo to tempt Brighton central defender Lewis Dunk into a second rash challenge, adding a second yellow card to the one he'd picked up in the first half. There was almost a goal from Aaron Mooy, who obliged when the crowd demanded he shoot from range after picking up the ball in acres of space, but he could only find the base of the post.

The ideal start to the month, Town didn't just solidify their play-off position, but legitimately made themselves the third party in a race for automatic promotion - the only side who proved themselves capable of keeping up with Brighton and Newcastle, who were otherwise untouchable. A win epitomised by the spirit shown by Aaron Mooy to make up for his mistake by cancelling out the goal he gave away by creating two others, Huddersfield thrived on the mentality of never knowing when they were beaten.

The arrival of Leeds came at an amusing time. Convinced themselves that they had the type of modern, sophisticated manager capable of returning them to where they believe they belong, the mood was as good there as it has been since their relegation from the top flight, all those years ago. With both sides full of confidence and wanting to play the game the right way, it was an interesting match on paper, with many expecting it to be far more open than it ended up being. While the football from David Wagner was all about forcing mistakes and making the most of them in the shortest amount of time possible, Leeds were more possession based, suffocating teams with the ball at their feet, before switching it into the final third and hoping the individual talent they had in attack was enough to convert the chances they made.

Leeds, in fact, actually had the first chance of the game, with Chris Wood forcing a smart stop from Danny Ward, having struck the ball across him from an acute angle. Town, who had started Collin Quaner up front in place of Nahki Wells, made several chances that their new forward ought to have done more with. The first, coming via a lovely through-ball from Kasey Palmer after some silky touches on the edge of the box, was hit straight at Rob Green, not causing the veteran keeper nearly enough of a problem. Palmer's last involvement in the game, he was forced off with a hamstring injury, so Izzy Brown was introduced in his place. A poor touch from Leeds in the left-back area gave Elias Kachunga an avenue to carry the ball down, and a recovering slide tackle from Pontus Jansson just gave the ball to Tommy Smith, who flashed it back where it came from first time, aiming at the six-yard box with pace. Anticipated perfectly by Izzy Brown, the loanee opened the scoring with a simple poke from close range, raising a single finger to his lips to silence the travelling support as he went.

Just under ten minutes later, however, Leeds were back on terms, and it was their main man Chris Wood who applied the finish. After a free kick was cleared by Town on the first attempt, the second ball ballooned into the box found the head of Kyle Bartley, who managed to cushion a headed pass to Wood alongside him. Being played onside by Michael Hefele, who hadn't cleared out in time after the first delivery, Wood juggled the ball around Ward in the air, before laying it into an open net. Many in the ground were under the impression that it was offside, because it had looked that way in real time, but cameras did prove afterwards that the equaliser was perfectly legitimate.

Within minutes of being brought to terms though, Huddersfield ought to have been ahead again. Thinking on the spot, Izzy Brown instinctively flicked a Jonathan Hogg volley around the corner, with the box still packed after an attacking corner had just broken down. Falling to the feet of Collin Quaner, whose first touch was a tad heavy, the German showed too much of the ball to Rob

Green, who was able to rush his feet and smother, before the shot could come off smoothly. From then on, Leeds retreated slightly, and allowed Huddersfield far more of the ball in the second half, which suited neither team. Although there was the odd half opening, nothing of note was being created, which did dampen the quality of the spectacle for much of the second period.

Right at the death, however, Town were probing down the left channel with Kachunga, when he turned back inside and found Aaron Mooy in space, who was urged to shoot from distance. Trying his luck, the Australian international somewhat scuffed his effort, which never really left the floor. Hit with some power, however, the Leeds right-back Luke Ayling instinctively turned a foot toward the ball as it flew at him, taking the ball from going harmlessly wide to straight across the goalmouth. Rob Green, who was at his near post expecting a strike, had to scramble back across, with Michael Hefele somehow unmarked on the edge of the six-yard box, with the ball flying toward him. Getting a side foot to the loose ball and turning it toward the left corner as Green dived in the other direction, pandemonium ensued. The stands were all limbs, screams and cheers, while on the pitch, Town were in much the same state. With players embracing on the floor while others gathered around Hefele - who didn't quite know what to do with himself at this point - David Wagner sprinted from his technical area across the field to celebrate with his players, unable to keep a cap on his emotions. Jumping on their backs and raising one fist to the air, Wagner looked more like a substitute than the manager, but it's for those moments that the crowd live to see.

Ending on a sour note, though, as Wagner made his way back to his area, Leeds coach Garry Monk made sure to step out into his path, causing a collision, and inspiring a scrum that involved both benches and sets of players, delaying the game for at least five minutes. What should have been a moment of joy quickly descended into farce, with Monk seemingly deciding to play the victim afterward, claiming that Wagner was purposefully trying to intimidate him. Both managers were sent to the stand as a result, and David Wagner was given a two-game touchline ban, meaning he would have to watch on from the stands while assistant Christoph Buhler prowled the technical area in his place. It would be remiss if we didn't highlight just how sanctimonious the behaviour Monk displayed was, having both been the cause of any issue and the one who made the biggest meal about it afterward. While it's true that Wagner shouldn't have entered the field of play to celebrate, he wasn't even looking in Monk's direction when he made his way back to the bench, and was outside the opposition technical area, too. Football is a sport often accused of becoming too commercially interested and sanitised for its own good, but it's in those moments - seeing a man so full of joy he sprints half a field to jump on his players after winning a game against their closest rivals in the final minute - that you remember what makes this sport great. Perhaps had Monk had his priorities straight, Leeds wouldn't have finished the season so poorly and missed out on the play-offs, and he might still be their manager, if he didn't walk out on them regardless anyway.

Given how that game ended on a personal note, the trip to Queens Park Rangers actually started on one. Their new manager, Ian Holloway, had started the season without a managerial job, so was employed by Sky to be their Championship expert. As part of that role, he predicted that Huddersfield would be relegated in 23rd place under David Wagner, and provided the following analysis as to why: "I haven't seen much progression from the club during the back end of last season. David

Wagner is pretty inexperienced and if results turn, then they may struggle to turn things around."

Naturally, given how well Huddersfield were doing, Ian Holloway turned into a figure of ridicule - despite later admitting he would never live down his error of judgement - and was the poster boy for the dismissive attitude that followed the club around for much of the season. People from Yorkshire are no strangers to having a bit of a chip on our shoulders, so when fans of other clubs were coming out with lines like: "we shouldn't be losing to teams like Huddersfield" - naturally, that became a motivating factor. David Wagner spoke at great length of how his club were punching about their weight, and how the terrier was a perfect symbol of that. The small dog - the underdog - always doing more than it's expected to, taking on bigger foes without a backward step, and backing itself in situations others wouldn't. Proving folk wrong became just as much of a prize as enjoying success, and it's something Dean Hoyle has never been shy of admitting works for him, too.

"It's fuel for me," admits Hoyle, honest as ever. "In business I always remember the competition saying to me never - he will never do it. All the way along, it is a chip on your shoulder, fuel for the fire and it does drive you on so you know, when I sold Card Factory, I always remember imagining Mr Clinton looking down on me one day and I thought right well I shafted you, up yours! These things do stick, so I actually don't mind people doubting us, because it works in our favour. Much like David does, talking up how much of an underdog we are. Sometimes it's not quite the full truth, but it works for us."

Funnily though, it's one area that David Wagner doesn't seem to echo his chairman's sentiments entirely, which is strange, given how much it did appear to sit with him.

"I don't think the team needed this as a motivation," he says, perhaps not wanting to make a bigger deal out of something than it already had been. "It was a help that maybe at the beginning over a long period of the season, the opponents underestimated us, until there was a moment where they thought, oh, maybe they are as good as they look. At the time when this happens, we were so confident and had so much trust and self belief in ourselves that even if they didn't underestimate us any longer, we were so good and so brave and so confident and had so much belief that we played good football.

Mentioning people by name was just to make a point, you know, look how far we've come!"

Those are thoughts that are echoed by Tommy Smith, who was Wagner's captain for much of the season.

"From the outside looking in, it would seem like that, like we had this chip on our shoulder - but it wasn't like that in reality, it wasn't like we've got something to prove or anything like that," he says, visibly shaking his head at the idea that detractors had in some way been a catalyst for their success. "It was all about knowing that we are what we are, and we're fine doing what we're doing. We made a big thing internally of people outside the football club being irrelevant to what we were doing. It was all about this is us, this is Huddersfield Town, doing what we're doing and seeing where it takes us. People have their opinions, but they certainly weren't going to have any effect on us, though. Holloway for example, a comment like that is not going to do anything. It was a case of brushing it off, and proving that things like that weren't going to affect us, which is how we achieved what we achieved. I think the manager still has that opinion now, that we achieved what we achieved because we were a team, and that's what made us strong, and it made us get to where we wanted to be. That's the way as a football club we like to conduct ourselves."

Of course, at QPR away, Town went two goals up midway through the first-half thanks to Izzy Brown and Nahki Wells, and carried that lead into the break. Even though the hosts pulled one back on the hour through Luke Freeman, it was never going to be enough to stop Town, who managed the game brilliantly, and could've won by more had they been sharper in the final third. The type of away game that had previously made the team come unstuck, these were the type of nonchalant wins that Huddersfield were now used to picking up, doing so with minimal fuss and all comfortably within their stride. As much to do with confidence as it is performance, having that air of difficulty about you is a hard thing to earn, but Huddersfield certainly weren't the top of anybody's list of teams to face.

In a different sort of a way, the next match, away to Rotherham, was another example of how that change in mentality manifests itself. Huddersfield twice fell behind to what was comfortably the worst side in the Championship, but despite that, the players on the pitch and the thousands of away fans in the stands didn't seem all that worried. There was a certain amount of inevitability about what was going to happen. After the second equaliser, which Kachunga scored with a bizarre header from point blank range, Town had around 15 minutes to win the game, but spent most of their time messing about with the ball, failing to put pressure on and letting Rotherham off the hook when they had them on the brink. Deep into added time, the ball was played in down the left channel at pace, with Jack Payne having to scruffily hook it back across to keep it from going out of play. Landing past Kachunga, who did stick out a foot for it, it bounced into the path of Tommy Smith on the edge of the box, who hit it first time on the half volley right back from where it came from, firing into the bottom corner. The goalkeeper didn't even move his feet.

Wheeling away, Smith did a lap of the entire away end celebrating, with Town seemingly unable to stop winning football matches. Just as much as that wasn't always the case, Smith's fan-favourite and captain status wasn't always a given, either, with his pre-Wagner form bringing him in for some stick. There was talk that during the summer Town may look to invest in a new right-back to complete their defensive remodelling, but David Wagner had never identified that as a problem area, because he thought he could help turn Tommy Smith into exactly the type of right-back he was after. Speaking to Smith about how his career has changed, it's clear that becoming comfortable in and of himself is at the heart of his improvement.

"I think there were always going to be people who are after your shirt, always going to be competition, that's the way the game is and I know that," he says, having been asked how Town bringing in another right-back may have affected him. "I'm experienced enough to know there's always other people who want to take your place, but it's up to me to stand up and say, this is my position. I've got this shirt. I think it's got to be earned on the pitch and I've just been myself. I'm at an age now that I feel I've done all my learning in terms of technical and skill, so I back my own ability - I always have done and I always will do as a player."

I was interested to know, having heard people openly doubt him in seasons gone by, what it's like to have gone from a player people ask to be replaced to one they openly celebrate, and are proud to call their captain. Does that leave a grudge, at all? "No, not in the slightest, because fans are entitled to their opinion, they pay their money, they go to the game, they only speak up because they care about the club. That never changes, that's football, some people like you, some won't, some will think you're great one week when you've won and the next thing ... you know as well as I do, football is a fickle sport. The individual accolade I received was special for me and I was grateful to receive that, a big thanks goes to my team-mates and the staff but in terms of showing fans who may've doubted me or whatever, that was irrelevant - some fans like you, some fans don't. All I need to do is try my best and go from there.

"It is nice and refreshing when a new manager comes to a football club and tells you exactly what he thinks of you as a player and a person," he says of David Wagner, who he clearly enjoys a good relationship with. "It gives you that push to think, okay, you have your own self belief, which is what I've got, and then the manager to come in and confirm that to you is a great feeling. When he tells you you can be better if you want to be better and you agree, it's about building that extra confidence and belief together, and it makes you want it even more. He's certainly been a big factor in what I've achieved personally over the last couple of years."

In a taste of what was to come in a tie against Manchester City in the FA Cup, there was no doubting where David Wagner had his priorities. With a game against play-off rivals Reading coming in just three days' time, Wagner played the same kind of changed side that took to the field against Port Vale and Rochdale, trusting those players to do themselves justice against the likes of Aguero, Nolito, Sane and De Bruyne, all of whom Guardiola gave significant minutes to. Despite playing most of the match without the ball, it was Town who had the better chances, and on another day, they may have nicked the win. Manchester City weren't ready for Huddersfield to be as fluid in transition, and found it difficult to adjust in the moments where they lost the ball. While they did dominate the statistics, they were poor on the day, and Guardiola made sure to highlight the professionalism of the Town outfit and sophistication of the tactics after the game. Holding a team like that to a scoreless draw was exceptional, especially with so many changes having been made, and it put some attention on Huddersfield and David Wagner that hadn't been there on a national scale previously.

What's likely to have made David Wagner happier than that draw, however, is that his rotation policy worked, and allowed him to field his strongest side against Reading at home, who'd quietly climbed their way up the table with Jaap Stam in charge. Playing a brand of possession based football with three at the back that Stam had adapted and brought with him from Ajax, it was the Reading work rate and their supreme organisation that stood them apart from most sides, as they rarely were playing risky enough football to make mistakes. The first game at Reading had been a close affair, and was only tipped in their favour after the needless red card for Van La Parra, so wasn't the fairest reflection of how they measured up against one another.

Split evenly right the way down the board in terms of possession, total shots, shots on target and fouls, it was only corners where Huddersfield had a clear advantage, although they were definitely the better team to watch with the ball at their feet. There is a saying in boxing that styles make fights, but where Stam and Wagner are concerned, their styles make for deeply tactical battles where each coach is trying to outwit the other, like chess. Awarded a penalty in the first half, a lack of clear instruction as to who should take the spot kick from Wagner meant that Rajiv van La Parra nominated himself, clearly attempting to atone for the first time these two sides had played. Taking a slow run up, he telegraphed where he was going to kick the ball, and did so in such a laid back manner that Ali Al-Habsi virtually caught the ball when it was kicked toward him. Wagner would later take the blame for that, saying that he had not made it clear enough that Christopher Lowe was the primary penalty taker, having only been awarded one other throughout the entire season.

For a short while after the penalty miss, Town did let their heads drop, and it was in that ten minutes where Reading were at their most dangerous. Huddersfield did eventually take the lead late in the second half, when Philip Billing was the first to react to a loose ball that was palmed back into danger by the goalkeeper, volleying it home from close range with less than ten minutes left to play. Town did make the better chances, and also Danny Ward was forced to tip one strike on to the bar, Reading weren't a great threat in the final third, and did their best work keeping the ball away from Huddersfield, and playing sensibly enough to not be caught out by the high press, which had been the end for most possession based teams. The win moved Huddersfield further clear of Reading, who would have leapfrogged Town with a win, and within four points of automatic promotion, which was still very much on the cards.

Bringing the mammoth month to an end away at Oakwell to face a robust Barnsley side, Town took an early lead through Michael Hefele, and wasted chances to extend their lead for the rest of the half. Adam Davies in the home goal had an absolutely brilliant game, and without him, the game may have been out of site for Huddersfield, but they couldn't quite keep that winning streak going. Izzy Brown, for example, had two efforts miraculously cleared off the line, so there was nothing more they could've done to extend their lead than what was attempted already. Barnsley came back into the match more in the second period, and were probably the better side when Marley Watkins popped up after 75 minutes to level the score, but they went back into their shell after, happy to defend and frustrate their way to a point against what was clearly a far superior outfit.

Given how pivotal February was built up to be, to come out of that undefeated across all competitions, having only dropped points once in six games in the league with an away draw, there's no reasonable way to have realistically expected much more from them. Much like how August set up their first half of the season for success, February did the same for the second - there's no quantifying just how important that might've been in the long run.

CHAPTER EIGHT

TAKING THE SCENIC ROUTE

Given the importance of the upcoming Newcastle match with automatic promotion still hanging in the balance, Huddersfield could probably have done without an FA Cup replay against Manchester City disrupting their preparation for it. While a cup run is all well and good, there's no hiding from the fact that promotion was the priority - the changed sides David Wagner was playing in the cup was as much a sign of that as anything. That said, however, the first leg was a great sign that, despite not playing their key talent, the system and ideology that Wagner had put in place was of a high enough standard to stifle even the most talent-rich club in the country. While there was some hope that those players could repeat that performance and perhaps play themselves within reaching distance of the final, most people expected Pep Guardiola to learn from his mistakes in the first leg, give Huddersfield the respect they deserve, and ensure his side made the gulf in individual star talent available count.

Having rotated slightly for the trip to Huddersfield, there was nothing of the sort from Manchester City in front of the television cameras at home. Sergio Aguero, Leroy Sane, Raheem Sterling and Kevin De Bruyne all started, signalling that the Premier League giants weren't about to let Town get away with another one. Consistent as ever, David Wagner named an extremely similar side to the one that almost won the first leg, keeping his first team regulars back for the upcoming league game.

For all their available talent, however, it was Huddersfield again who started the brighter, and thanks to wonderful, intelligent play from Philip Billing in the midfield, Harry Bunn was able to squirm through an opening goal to silence the crowd after just 7 minutes. Having been on the books at City in his youth team days, it will have been an especially sweet moment for Bunn to be the one to kick the hornet's nest and get the opening goal. Billing, who was brilliant in the first leg, too, was showing his ability against a midfield that consisted of Fernandinho and De Bruyne, showing a remarkable lack of fear for one with such limited experience in matches of that stature. Standing at 6'5 going on 6'6, he looks more like an oversized basketball guard than a creative midfielder, but he uses that length and size to his advantage, shielding the ball well, and beating players with short sharp bursts of long strides, in a manner that isn't too dissimilar to Yaya Toure, who's obviously towards the top of that particular tree.

Manchester City would go on to score three goals in eight minutes before the break, and added two more for good luck before full-time, but for Huddersfield, the performance of Billing was the real story, and enough of a positive to make that experience seem worth it.

There aren't, in truth, many players who can do what Billing can. Excellent with either foot, smart playing short or just as accurate when spraying balls across over longer distances, his appreciation for touch, space and timing are far beyond his years. While there are still some inconsistencies given his age, that's no reason to discount his obvious talent. To be able to run a game from a withdrawn position whilst still contributing on a defensive front is a precious commodity in the modern game, but it's a role Billing is tailor-made for. Before the game at the Etihad is over, Billing again shows his ability and vision by playing Joe Lolley through with a ball that's probably even better than the first, but it isn't given the finish it deserves. It's hard to come out of a game with any credit when your side has just been pumped 5-1, but that's exactly what the young Dane did, cementing himself as Huddersfield's most exciting young player in the process.

Having all but folded against Manchester City, knowing the Newcastle game was coming shortly afterwards, Town fans can't be blamed for getting their hopes up, with the club clearly having singled this game out as their primary chance to disrupt the automatic promotion race, and perhaps bypass the play-off process altogether. Having been outmanoeuvred earlier in the season by Wagner, however, Rafa Benitez was never going to make this game easy for Huddersfield, and he effectively set out his side as he would in a knockout game in European competition, trying to keep his defence as compact as possible, but have the pace and skill in the areas required to nick an away goal should the chance present itself.

In the midst of an excellent unbeaten run in the league, there wasn't a chance in hell that Huddersfield were going to do anything but go for the win from the very first minute, especially after the joy they got against Brighton employing a similar intensity and tactic. Unfortunately for them, though, that's exactly what Newcastle were prepared for them to do, and Rafa Benitez paid David Wagner and his men the ultimate respect by conceding that, and finding a way around Town, just as he would against the biggest names in the Premier League, which is how he spent the majority of his coaching career at the highest level.

Huddersfield's first loss in seven games in the league, and only their second of 2017, it was a difficult blow to take. The early penalty for Newcastle looked to have more than a hint of dive behind it, with Matt Ritchie finding the deck with incredible ease, despite there being some inconsequential and accidental contact. The former Bournemouth man picked himself up and converted the penalty, putting his side in front after only ten minutes. Their second, which came after half an hour, was also shrouded in controversy, with Huddersfield keeper Danny Ward claiming to have had the ball in control in two hands when Daryl Murphy dispossessed him and finished into an empty net. Just as in the case of the penalty, the referee wasn't interested in hearing the other side of the argument.

Giving some fight back themselves, Town were awarded a penalty of their own just after the 70-minute mark, with Elias Kachunga clumsily bundled over by Jonjo Shelvey, despite him having absolutely nowhere to turn at the time of the foul. Aaron Mooy, cool as ever, sent the goalkeeper the wrong way as he halved the deficit from the spot. More than happy to sit deep and defend their lead for the rest of the match, Huddersfield couldn't find a way through for the equaliser, try as they might. Leaving themselves open at the back in order to throw as many bodies forward as possible towards the end of the game, Town were undone in added-on time by a simple long ball up the field, which substitute goalkeeper Joel Coleman - who came on at half-time after Danny Ward suffered a knock - misjudged the flight of, allowing Dwight Gayle to skip through unchallenged, with an open goal to walk the ball into.

A crushing way to lose, especially with the prospect of automatic promotion all but ended by the result, the trick for Wagner was to make sure that result didn't knock their confidence or belief too heavily, with a result and a statement of intent needed in their next game to underline their mental fortitude in the face of disappointment. One loss is one loss - to allow it to become more than that is where the real trouble sets in.

Given the schedule in the Championship, there wasn't long to dwell on that loss, which is probably a blessing in disguise. With a heavily invested-in Aston Villa side now lead by Steve Bruce due at the John Smith's just three days after the Newcastle fixture, complacency could not be afforded or tolerated. After abandoning their failed experiment with Roberto Di Matteo before it had even begun - and failing to poach David Wagner in the aftermath - Steve Bruce was attempting to spend his way up the division, having made six high profile signings in the January window alone.

The game itself was fairly even, but Town were clearly the better side, and were showing their extra quality in short bursts of dominance, without ever making it count. Still somewhat stilted after that earlier loss, it took some time before they looked properly comfortable in their own skin again. Villa appeared to be trying to leave Albert Adomah with chances to run at Chris Lowe in isolation, but they had no luck targeting one of the division's most consistent full-backs. An unspoken and unsung hero of that Town backline, Lowe is a thoroughly tenacious player with a bit of a hidden mean streak in him, as he's not one to shy away from chipping off when the occasion calls for it, or going in particularly hard against somebody who he might prefer to slow down a little when they're in his area of the park. An excellent signing during the summer, not enough is said about Lowe, who tends to keep a low profile away from the field - no pun intended.

That said, though, it was Town's other full-back that ended up winning the game, with a short corner actually leading to something, for once. A move that looked to have been designed in training, Mooy cut the ball back to Smith on the edge of the area in space. Skipping past the one man who'd read the move by shaping to play the ball first time in the opposite direction, Smith then dropped his shoulder and carried it around him down the right hand channel, suddenly finding himself in space within shooting distance with no defensive cover around him.

Backing himself in much the same manner as he did against Rotherham, the Town skipper hit across the ball aiming for the far corner, whipping the ball back in on itself from an awkwardly acute angle to ensure it found the side netting with as little fuss as possible. Although it's not something he'd ever say or admit to, there must've been some desire for David Wagner to show the one domestic club who'd come for him why he decided to stay in Huddersfield, and that victory went some way to explaining why first-hand. A definite bonus on top of the much needed three points.

Backed up by another 1-0 win, this time away at Brentford, it was a performance reminiscent of their trip to QPR not long before - going in professionally to get the job done, not allowing the opposition to play their game and disrupt their momentum. It was good to see that maintained and not just a one-off, as it would be the perfect mindset to get themselves into ahead of most away trips. The game was won thanks to a deflected effort from Rajiv van La Parra, who divides the opinion of Town fans more than most. A player of undoubted quality with the ball at his feet and incredible to watch in full flight, it's just the consistency of his final product and penchant to do something daft like get sent off for dissent that take away from what a nuttily exciting player he is. Underrated defensively, too, his tracking back and support of his full-back are regularly second to none, and shouldn't be overlooked. It's those minor details that will be keeping him in David Wagner's side, not deflected goals or step overs.

Having recovered so well post Newcastle, there was an outside chance of automatic promotion again, but Town would have to come through an away game against Bristol City first, before even thinking of that as a possibility again.

Just as Town were settling into the game, however, Jonathan Hogg went down clutching his neck after an awkward collision with Mark Hudson, having seemingly bent his head the wrong way after running face first into his captain's torso by mistake. A scary scene to see on the field, especially with a warrior of a man like Hogg the victim, the medical staff took around fourteen minutes to move Hogg and secure him properly to the stretcher, with the immediate fear being serious neck or spinal damage. Shaken by that, it wasn't long before Bristol City took the lead, with Lee Tomlin providing the breakthrough. Offering nothing up top and unravelling at the back, Huddersfield went on to lose 4-0 in a game where Bristol City weren't even that great. With their pace causing the Town defence problems through the middle, Mark Hudson came in for criticism after the defeat, with the suggestion being that he was no longer of the right level to represent Huddersfield, with some suggesting that his legs may have gone.

Hudson smiles when that's brought up to him now, and is as politically correct as ever when offering his reply. "That's part and parcel of being a professional - everyone's got their right to their opinion," he says, being the bigger man and not giving further attention to those who make it their business to spread negativity.

"It wouldn't affect whether I was playing well or not playing well, because I've taken criticism throughout my career and learnt how to deal with it," he continues. "I'm able to take that and not let that drift back into the dressing room. I think it's just who I am. Being the captain is great, but as a person, I'm capable of taking that on the chin. You have to be that sort of character to say, that's fine. I understand that in football people have opinions, whether it's right or wrong, you're entitled to it."

In truth, the Bristol game was a rare start for Hudson, with both Hefele and Stankovic unavailable. As he seems to with most things, there's a level of understanding behind his attitude to these changes, which comes with experience.

"Obviously given who was playing more, Michael Hefele was pushing in training well and really going for the start, and maybe my form dropped too. I got injured as well around that time, so that wasn't a help. He came in and played well so it was never an issue for me to say, why am I not playing? I'm not the person to have an issue, if someone's coming in and doing it well then I'll wait. I had conversations with the boss about it, we talked it through and that's part of mine and the boss's relationship really, that we're open with each other. He explained his reasons and I accept them, so from then on it's obviously down to me to maintain my levels and training, so if I'm not playing I'm still someone people can rely on to look at and look for advice and keep the group together and tight."

Did the loss of his place effect his ability to be a leader within the squad? He was still the club captain, but Tommy Smith was wearing the armband far more regularly than he was. "No, I don't think so," he says, trying to think back if there were any teething problems or awkwardness as he answers. "Just generally as a captain, you have to be reliable - regardless of how you play, whether you win or lose - you have to be reliable off the pitch and on it. You have to maintain a level where people can approach you whether you're playing well or not playing well. You have to take your own performance away from your mind, whether people see that as you being a captain, you have to be a bit selfless. Your job is to be there for everybody else in the group."

In the grander scheme of things, that loss all but confirmed Huddersfield's inability to catch Brighton and Newcastle in the automatic promotion places, so the plan had to now change - cement a place in the top six, and make sure you're over the line and ready for the play-offs.

CHAPTER NINE:

OVER THE LINE

That whole cementing a play-off berth plan didn't start the greatest in April, with Burton somehow coming to the John Smith's Stadium and leaving with all three points, leaving most people dumbfounded as to how. Far from a good side, and definitely not sophisticated in their approach, Burton actually leaned into their limitations and decided to embrace their weaknesses. That's the nice way of saying they defended deep and kicked absolute lumps out of Town whenever they got anywhere near to their area, with the referee somehow blind to what was going on. Capitalising on Town's somewhat fragile state after the disappointment at losing in Bristol in the fashion they did, and the knock-on effect of that in terms of the top two - Burton just simply made hay while the sun shone. You can't really begrudge them that.

With just four days to pick themselves up for the visit of Norwich, there was no time for a blip at this time in the season. With teams on the outskirts of the top six putting together their late runs to get inside it before the season finishes, Huddersfield would have to make sure of keeping themselves safe enough to stay on those positions, or the season really will have ended on the most sour not possible. Given how they responded in the next game, though, it's clear that they already knew that much.

Unlike in the away game, the first half of this fixture was far more calm and measured than it had been at Carrow Road, with Town still trying to recapture that zip and belief that had propelled them up the league in the first place. Huddersfield, however, did have their own unexpected bonus in midfield, with Jonathan Hogg returning from what was initially a suspected broken neck in just a matter of weeks. Having consulted specialists that clarified what was misdiagnosed from his initial x-rays, the club medical staff were satisfied that Hogg could be released for full participation again. Playing with a renewed sense of purpose, Hogg was operating under the impression that his season would be over, and with an injury as serious as the one that was suspected, there was some speculation over whether or not he'd be able to safely play again. The type of man who will literally stick his head where others wouldn't dare their boot, though, if anybody was going to defy the medical experts in that sort of manner, it was always going to be him.

In the second half, however, Town looked transformed. With the click of a finger, the smiles appeared back on the faces, the pace was back in their passing and pressing, and all of a sudden, Norwich didn't look so comfortable any more. Lead in part by Elias Kachunga, the striker turned winger was an inspired signing in the summer, finishing the season Town's top scorer for the season. Tireless both with and without the ball, the partnership he formed with Tommy Smith became a highlight of the season, and was the route to victory more than once. The secret to their success, Kachunga's ability to drift inside without being followed, was a stroke of genius, and the basis of so many Huddersfield goals.

Essentially, by allowing Smith to overlap and stepping inside as if he was a passing option, Kachunga would often lose his man marker, leaving him free to take up a position in the centre of the box that the defence wasn't prepared enough to defend. He wasn't just Town's main right-place-right-time man - he was more right place, right time, better approach. Again, it was that right wing partnership that opened the scoring for Town, with Smith playing a ball over the top for Kachunga to somehow latch on to, before finishing past the keeper from a difficult angle. Not the smartest goal they'd ever scored, it was one of the most important, and Kachunga's willingness to chase lost causes was once again coming up trumps.

Once they were ahead, Huddersfield added goals two and three within ten minutes of the first. Aaron Mooy scored the second, finding the bottom corner from close range after some neat interplay inside the box, and Wells made sure of the win with the weakest goal of the lot, passing a tame left-footed shot through the Norwich keeper, who didn't shower himself in glory for any of the three goals, to be perfectly honest. At the other end of the field, though, Christopher Schindler deserves praise for being a constant source of good in defence for Town, no matter if the rest of the team are functioning to full capacity or not. Clearly one of the best central defenders in the division - if not the best - he's too humble a character to be drawn on that when asked. Avoiding that question, he'd rather discuss the rigours of the Championship schedule, and how that rules everything the club do throughout the season.

"There are so many things said about football players these days," he says, trying to deflect by making a wider point. "I don't read articles and newspapers about individual performances. I just try to do my best and do my job in the squad the entire year - that's all I ask of myself. It's so tough to be at your best all the time when there are so many different styles you face, and so many opponents you play against - maybe a tall striker first, then you play opponents with a quick mobile striker - it's not easy to be the same against every type, because if you say you are, you're calling yourself the best defender in the world. I don't want to do that.

"In the Championship," he continues, still trying to tell me why he isn't as good as we think he is - or at least, doing his best not to acknowledge that question - "where games are coming so quick and at such volumes, it happens that you drop a game here and there. For us, there was also learning to be done about English football, but the squad last season was so tight in their quality that you can easily rotate players. Every single player was replaceable with another of the same level. That was a big advantage we had, that maybe if we had some players who were tired because of the number of games, you can swap and rotate. It was good that we also had those crucial games where we won in the last minute. This was some kind of special season I think, now or never."

To prove his point, Town followed up their big win over Norwich by going to relegation-threatened Nottingham Forest and losing 2-0 fairly comfortably, never really being able to get a foothold in the game. With the end of the season closing in and Town suddenly losing that buffer they'd built between themselves and those before the play-offs, they couldn't afford to be making losses like this a regularity, despite all the difficulties Schindler outlined about trying to compete to the highest level across 46 gruelling games. Only a couple of wins away from mathematically securing their play-off place, there was some nervous weeks at this point in the season, wondering just how long Town could afford to go before sewing up their finishing place.

Putting the Nottingham loss behind them, Huddersfield then engaged in one of the most entertaining home games of the season, with Preston North End volunteering themselves as pantomime villains in a five goal thriller. Opening the scoring against the run of play thanks to a solo run and strike by Aiden McGeady, his strike from distance was one of the finest the John Smith's saw all season. That man Elias Kachunga brought Town level before half-time, and then on the 70th minute mark, young Jack Payne managed to get Huddersfield into the lead for the first time. Things aren't ever that easy though, are they? Having been chipping off all game and making himself an easy target for the more boisterous Town fans in the stands, Jordan Hugill equalised for Preston in the 79th minute, appearing to deny Huddersfield what would've been a well fought win, and ideal response to the lethargic loss at Nottingham.

Luckily for Town, though, Hugill wasn't done. Caught throwing Elias Kachunga to the floor in the penalty box in an off the ball incident by the linesman, referee Lee Probert made a massive call, awarding Town a spot kick deep into injury time. With the Preston players protesting their cause, it was a full five minutes, at least, between the kick being awarded and taken, by which time it was definitely going to be the last action of the game. Aaron Mooy was to take it after converting his last one against

Newcastle, and he struck the ball cleanly toward the right hand side of the goal, only to see his effort saved by Chris Maxwell in the Preston goal, who managed to parry the ball back out into danger. Having reacted the quickest, Collin Quaner met the saved penalty first, passing it in the bottom corner past the goalkeeper before a defender could get themselves in the way. Sparking some of the wildest celebrations of the season, Quaner ran half the length of the Kilner Bank before being caught by his team-mates, who swamped him.

Perversely, while that win didn't confirm their play-off spot, it did keep their dim hopes of automatic promotion alive, with a top two finish still not mathematically ruled out. Just three days later, Collin Quaner picked up against Derby where he left off against Preston, scoring after just nine minutes at Pride Park, getting on the end of a Martin Cranie cross with a tidy finish. Town had to win to deny Brighton confirmation of their automatic promotion, but former Town midfielder Jacob Butterfield levelled the score at the death, confirming Brighton's promotion as he went. One of many to have left Huddersfield in recent seasons with designs on finding a more realistic club to be promoted with, Butterfield and Derby finished a full 17 points adrift of the top six, which is about as clear an illustration as you can get about what players used to think of Huddersfield before David Wagner took over, and where they are in comparison afterward.

Fulham, the division's in form team, were next up at the John Smith's, but Town actually hit the front against the run of play inside five minutes, when Chris Lowe was brought down for a penalty, before getting up and converting it himself. That was about as good as it got for Huddersfield on the day, though - Fulham scored four goals before half-time, completely killing the game. Scott Malone scored first halving the deficit, before a Tom Cairney penalty completed the turnaround. Stefan Johansen would score two more alone before the break, rendering the second half a non-event. Having beaten Huddersfield in similar fashion 5-0 at Craven Cottage, it clearly wasn't a match-up that suited Town, and one they were keen to avoid should they manage to confirm their play-off status. The speed with which Fulham were able to break and score with relative ease is where they looked most scary, especially when they've so many players across the field who've an eye for goal.

With automatic promotion finally ruled out, Huddersfield

travelled to Wolverhampton knowing that a win would guarantee them a place in the play-offs, which is what they'd spent all season working toward. No team had spent more time in the top six than Huddersfield that season, so it only seemed fair that Town would get the opportunity to compete and show what they were all about. Somewhat staggering across the line rather than sprinting across it confidently, this 1-0 away win at Wolves would be Huddersfield's only win in the last five league games of the season. Izzy Brown scored the breakthrough goal from distance after half an hour at Molineux, and that proved enough in the end, moving the side eight points clear of seventh with only two games left to play. Celebrating their achievement with the away support that night, the significance of the win wasn't lost on anyone connected with Huddersfield Town, either inside or outside the club - they were now in touching distance of the Premier League.

All but forfeiting their last two games of the season, David Wagner was fined by the EFL for the number of changes he made for a 2-0 loss away at Birmingham City, rotating the side much in the same fashion he had been doing without complaint all season. In their final home game of the regular season, Cardiff put three past a Town team who looked like they were trying to conserve energy and not get injured before the play-offs started. That memo might not have made it all the way to Danny Ward though, as early in the first half, he came rushing out of his area to stop a Cardiff counter, and ended up handling the ball outside of the box. A straight red card that there was no arguing, he would miss the first leg of whatever play-off Huddersfield were drawn in, which was never part of the plan.

It was interesting speaking to Dean Hoyle about his feelings when the top six finish was earned, because rather than think about the achievement, he said instead he remembered most what the club was like before that season, and how the whole conversation had now changed for the better. Identity, claims the chairman, is what got Huddersfield where they are, but before the arrival of David Wagner, he's not sure the football club actually had one that anyone understood, or subscribed to.

"I remember, when Stuart Webber first came on board, he told me that the problem with Huddersfield is, you could watch them play for years, and you didn't know if they were going to turn out in a 4-4-2, 4-2-3-1 or a 3-5-

2. Did they play long ball, or keep it short without losing the ball - what on earth are we going to do? Nobody knew. All that changed when David came in, playing that full throttle brand of the game. It was exactly what we needed."

Before the season had started, I put it to Wagner that he seemed confident during pre-season, happy with his signings and well on his way to getting the players up to speed with how he wanted the game played. The topic of finishing top six came up and he laughed in my face. Reminding him of this over a year later, I wondered, did you really have an inclination at that point, or was he playing smart with me?

"No!" he laughs, when I suggest he might have lied to me. "I don't have to say something different to the outside to what I really think. I thought to myself, if we go from where we started, which is when we finished 19th, I thought if this team can finish in 12th, it will be a very good achievement from my point of view. Again, we took over one or two points above the drop zone, and after our first two defeats we were actually in the drop zone. This was why I said top ten or top six, this is not realistic for a football club of our size with our budget with the circumstance we have even at this time. We're not in a circumstance where we can say we're a Championship club who's able to chase for the top six or top then. I was telling the truth, not lying - this is the reason why I laughed!"

CHAPTER TEN:

NO LIMITS

There were just seven days between Huddersfield's last game of the regular season and the first leg of their play-off semi-final against Sheffield Wednesday at home. Having been confident of finishing within the play-off places for some time, David Wagner had begun to rotate his side and allow them to play with less intensity than we were used to, the assumption being that Huddersfield would get their rest in early, hoping to be as fresh as possible for whoever they would face come the end of the season. Obviously, it was an early boost to have avoided Fulham, who handed Town two of their worst defeats of the season, but Town hadn't exactly shone against Wednesday, either.

A tense affair from start to finish, neither side could claim to have really made any clear cut chances, although there was one half chance where Nahki Wells could've perhaps done better against Keiren Westwood, who did well to make himself big. Given that Huddersfield were defending so well, Wednesday were largely reduced to having speculative shots from range, which is obviously how they beat Town at Hillsborough, thanks to a Ross Wallace special. In truth, the game sort of passed by once both teams knew neither was going to take the initiative in attack, and there seemed to be a mutual appreciation that they would see this out in the second leg, with neither party looking to go into that game at an aggregate disadvantage.

Huddersfield did what they could with the majority of the ball that was given to them, but statistics of almost 70% possession don't tend to happen unless one side has proactively decided to play without the ball. Wednesday didn't manage one shot on target, while Town had two, which paints a picture of just how little action was happening around both sets of goals. A strange decision by Carvalhal, given that Danny Ward was missing - you would have assumed that he may have seen Joel Coleman as a target on such an occasion, but Town's second choice stopper was more a spectator and a ball boy than anything else.

Speaking after the game, David Wagner alluded to how deep Wednesday had set up, leaving his side no option but to play in front of them, not wishing to overplay their hand, as that's exactly what Carlos Carvalhal appeared to be banking on. He told the press: "I'm happy with the performance. We have shown we are a competitor. I wish we got a victory because I think if one team deserved it, it was my team. Unfortunately, we were not able to use one of the chances that we had. We dominated the opponent and we shouldn't forget they are one of the best defensive teams in the division. We had a good balance and they had more or less no chances. I have no idea what they will do on Wednesday and I am not worried about it. I'm not sure how their supporters will react if they play that deep at home, but I'm not worried."

Sadly, the first half of the second leg was much the same as the entirety of the first had been, with Wednesday still refusing to take ownership of the occasion, even in their own stadium. While the South Yorkshire club did have more possession this time around and certainly did more to trouble the goalkeeper, it was still Huddersfield who made the better chances, with Izzy Brown missing an amazing chance to make it 1-0 early in the game after putting his first time effort just wide, clipping the post as it went.

Finally playing with some sense of urgency, Wednesday picked it up in the second period, and were rewarded for doing so almost immediately. Picking the ball up in a fairly deep position away to the left, Scottish international Barry Bannan hit a wonderful early cross into the box, with Steven Fletcher on hand to bury his header, the first time he'd really been given a proper sniff of the goal. Knowing the trouble Town had in scoring, Wednesday went back to playing within themselves again, confident that they had enough to defensively to keep Huddersfield quiet. It did take Huddersfield a minute or two to regain composure after falling behind, and they didn't start to look dangerous until Elias Kachunga was substituted for Collin Quaner on the 72nd minute mark.

Despite scoring and assisting on his debut in the cup, tapping in the last minute winner against Preston and opening the scoring against Derby away, there weren't many fans too sure of Collin Quaner, who'd been in and out of the side since his January move. Occasionally questionable with the first touch and unfortunate enough to have had his least impressive performances when the television cameras have been there previously, there was some concern that the move simply wasn't going to work out. However, within a minute of being introduced, Izzy Brown played an inch perfect through ball in behind the Wednesday defence for him to run on to inside the box. Electing to pass rather than shoot, his ball went via a combination of Nahki Wells and Tom Lees into the back of the net, bringing Huddersfield back on terms. For the rest of the game, Quaner looked like Town's best outlet, using his pace and power to create an absolute nightmare of a situation for the Wednesday full-back tasked with marking him.

In extra time, chances were tight, but either side did have one good effort each. First, for Wednesday, former Town forward Jordan Rhodes broke confidently into the box, but could only shoot straight at Danny Ward, who parried his uncharacteristically rushed strike away. At the Town end, a second chance ball after a fairly poor corner fell to Wells who did the hard part of making himself the room to shoot, but only hit the side netting.

Before long, it became inevitable that spot kicks were going to be the only way to separate the sides.

Huddersfield were to take first, with Chris Lowe handed the ball. Stood with it under his arm waiting while Keiren Westwood went through his time-wasting techniques, he made no mistake when it came time to step up. Curling the ball hard with his instep into the bottom right corner, Westwood went the right way, but couldn't get close to an expertly hit pen. Sam Hutchinson was to take next, having his tame tap down the centre right beaten away by Ward, who managed to hold his position and read the penalty exactly. Michael Hefele was next for Huddersfield, but seemed to take an age to place the ball, before starting his run up somewhere outside the penalty area. Turning the face of his boot on to the ball at the last minute, the German centre half calmly rolled the ball into the right hand corner of the goal, with the keeper guessing the wrong way. Celebrating by firing an imaginary arrow on his way back to the centre circle, he would later explain that as Robin Hood, he was stealing from the rich - Sheffield Wednesday - and giving to the poor - Huddersfield Town.

Barry Bannan would soon equalise for Wednesday in the shootout, sparking a run of Nahki Wells, Kieran Lee, Aaron Mooy and Jack Hunt all scoring with little drama. Having volunteered to take Town's fifth with the chance to win it in his hands, Jack Payne made his way up from halfway. Placing the ball down with little fuss and puffing his cheeks out as he took his steps backward, he opted for power over placement, and have his strike saved at an almost identical place as Hutchinson saw his blocked, too. Payne immediately had his head in his hands, while Keiren Westwood got the chance to puff out his chest and celebrate with the fans, who had all just breathed a collective sigh of relief.

Needing to score to keep Wednesday in it, their star forward Fernando Forestieri stepped forward, safe in the knowledge that he'd already beaten Danny Ward twice this season - once from the penalty spot, and the other from open play. Opting for a burst of short steps in his run up in the image of Roberto Carlos, he too went for power over placement, and got the same result. Ward flew across to his right, getting his full body behind the ball, keeping it out in the most emphatic manner possible. Smashing the ball back into the now empty net, Forestieri was the last man Wednesday fans would've expected to let them down.

Danny Ward, who takes a good five to ten seconds to twig that it's all done and over, suddenly sets off on the mother of all adrenaline fuelled sprints, charging toward the Huddersfield fans at the other end of the stadium, with the rest of the players and staff behind him, struggling to keep up. Once the singing had died down and the hugging stopped, the players and staff all linked arms, and celebrated with the travelling fans as only they know how. Not wanting to let his players leave the field without speaking on their achievement, and looking ahead at what was to come, a huddle formed around David Wagner, who was wagging one finger in the air and bellowing the same three words: "One more game."

Huddersfield Town - forever relegation fodder with the fourth lowest budget in the Championship and a manager who'd never taken full charge of a professional senior side before - were going to Wembley, to play Reading for the right to be a Premier League club. All they had to do was win it, now...

With a two-week gap between their game and the final at Wembley, it was decided before the semi-final that, should they win, they would disappear on a week away in Portugal, to spend time with the families as a group again, and train in warm weather.

"He's more demanding," Dean Hoyle says of his coach, when I asked how he felt about paying out for another week away in the sun for the whole group. "He expects certain standards, but I'm not one to say no because everything that he's done, he's done for a reason. I always talk about small percentages - if you get 5% more right, you get 5% improvement on the pitch. That's right the way down to the small things, too. He once asked me, why do we drive to a game? Because instead, he wanted the players to come in at 10am, get them a coach, get them a hotel, and then we'll leave together. They will come to the game at 1.30pm on the coach together, rather than turning up one by one. Little things like that make a huge difference. I look at it as the chairman and think, that makes sense. He's very clear, very methodical - you'd think he was German, or something."

The idea behind going away was the same as it was originally, when David organised that week in Marbella, just as he joined the club. This time around, however, there was the added bonus of keeping the players away from the excitement and pressure building in the town, the requests from journalists and photographers - allowing them to concentrate on themselves, training, recovery and their families, away from all the other distractions. There would be plenty of time for all that later. What's most fascinating, though, is to hear Wagner discuss the adjustments he made in training with Wembley and Reading in mind specially:

"We didn't change training completely, but we do adjust things in regards to a certain opposition, so certain drills and activities are designed thinking forward to a certain opponent. We changed our training pitch to the same size as the pitch at Wembley to make everyone aware that it was only half a yard different, it only looks bigger than that. We left our usual lines painted as well but we made them a little bit darker than the Wembley lines in white, just so they could see how small the difference is. It's nearly exactly the same size, so it isn't something that's extraordinary, and I wanted to make them aware of that. Even if the size of the ground and atmosphere will be extraordinary, the pitch isn't.

"We worked on our set up against the three back line, which Reading used the majority of the time. We looked at how we want to attack them, how we want to defend them with the player shape they had. We didn't work on that until the week before the game, though, because I didn't want to leave such a big gap between those sessions and the final."

The most anticipated game in the modern history of Huddersfield Town, the demand for tickets to Wembley was higher than anyone had imagined. Speaking to Sue Beaumont, who runs the ticket office for the club, she gave us an insight into just how much work goes into organising sales for a game of that magnitude. "We were staggered at the numbers," she says, half laughing. "It was exceptionally busy, the busiest we've had. Our workload is tempered, we use agencies to help because with the time scale there is no way we can do it alone.

"Back when I first started, which is just about 25 years ago now, people came and queued for tickets, and bought twenty or thirty for a group at a time, but you can't do that now. Consequently, the workload here is completely different, we tend to deal with the players' tickets, hospitality area tickets and the coaches, which is a mammoth operation. We took nearly 100 coaches to Wembley, which was a lot to organise. It's a good problem to have, though. You want the success. I'd rather win and be busy than the alternative.

"As is the case across the club, we want to be as public facing and customer service orientated as possible. That's always been the case here, and success won't change that, I don't think. I've seen entire generations of families come through here, and you get to know people across time, too. That's a really fulfilling aspect of the job, to be honest. Seeing your hard work pay off."

Pay off it did - walking down Wembley Way on the day of the final, you couldn't move for Town fans. According to figures released to the club, they suggest just north of 30,000 people turned up to support Town that day, which is more than the John Smith's can hold at a time. The mood ahead of the game was jovial, rather than worrisome, and Reading made for pleasant opposition - it was nice seeing fans of opposition clubs sharing fan parks and designating areas that were designed to keep them apart, rather than any trouble starting. Walking into the stadium itself, the buzz was incredible - there was the same togetherness and shared belief in that stand at Wembley as there had been at the John Smith's Stadium all season. There didn't, in truth, seem to be anything of the sort coming from the Reading side.

The game itself, much like the semi-final, followed a

similar pattern as the league games did. Town, starting far faster, could've - maybe should've - been ahead on two separate occasions early on. Michael Hefele uncharacteristically missed what appeared to be a fairly free and fairly simple header wide, while Izzy Brown missed an almost identical chance to the one he got wrong at Hillsborough, in exactly the same way. Reading, reacting to this, closed themselves right up, not wanting Huddersfield to have the same openings again. While even one of those goals could've opened the game up, forced Reading out to chase the game and made the final far better for it, missing had the adverse effect - Reading were now a purely reactive team, not proactive in the slightest, and Town were going to have to find a way through that, rather than against a team looking to actually play some football against them.

For the rest of the game, it was cagey to watch. The sides split possession straight down the middle, had almost identical shooting statistics and even the same number of fouls and yellow cards - if you were looking to find a narrative in the statistical analysis, there wasn't one. With the game winding down, Kachunga - who still wasn't fully fit, but played regardless - made way for Quaner, but both coaches seemed resigned to extra time, so were keeping substitutions to themselves in anticipation. Right on the stroke of full-time, however, Town were forced into a change. Tommy Smith, captain's armband on, was making one last drive forward, looking to recreate one of those late winners he'd so much enjoyed earlier in the season. A covering tackle by a Reading player forced Smith to get as much of the floor as he did the ball, and the captain wasn't getting up as a result.

"I'm not normally one to touch wood," Smith tells me, knocking on the table next to him before he tells this part of the story, "because I'm very fortunate with injuries normally, so to go off in the manner I did in the final, biggest game of the year - it was really disappointing. I was more disappointed for the team that I couldn't help and be there, that I was off the pitch and couldn't influence anything. I had a boot on my foot. I almost felt helpless watching the end. I felt completely helpless. So desperate to get over the line. As a club and for the team and for the town, I was desperate to get over the line."

Martin Cranie would take his place and Jonathan Hogg would take the armband, but nothing much else would happen for the remainder of the game. There were half chances, nothing more, in added-on time, but it was clear for some time just how this game was going to be decided. Prayers had been going on in the stands in anticipation for some time already. It was going to be spot kicks again, and everybody knew it. What had been a party atmosphere in the Huddersfield end was suddenly becoming a little bit more subdued, as folk mentally prepared themselves for what was about to happen, and how their fate was going to be decided. Jonathan Hogg - acting as captain - saw the first coin toss decide that the penalties would be taken facing the Huddersfield fans, with the second being won by Chris Gunter, who elected for Reading to kick first.

Yann Kermorgant was the first man up, going with a short run up. Danny Ward stood opposite him, bouncing on his toes, making himself look big, smacking the crossbar with his hands - all the tricks available to a goalkeeper to get in the head of the kicker in these situations. Going low and hard into the left corner, Ward dived the right way, but wasn't even close to it. Chris Lowe was up first for Town and, not hanging around, stroked the ball with his instep, sending Al-Habsi the wrong way. Danny Williams was next up - perhaps Reading's best player on the day - and he walked up to his kick and rolled it down the centre of the goal, away from Ward who had again dived to his right. Michael Hefele came up next, in the same order as they had against Sheffield Wednesday, but he visibly wasn't fully fit. Having gone down several times with cramp and in the midst of playing through an Achilles injury severe enough that would delay his start to the following season, hit a weak penalty down the keeper's right, and Al-Habsi had it covered all day long. Having missed, Town had to come back from behind.

Liam Kelly walked up next for Reading, and he seemed nervous from the stand. Still just a teenager, it was an immense amount of pressure for him to be putting himself through - but that never showed during his kick. Lacing it down the middle into the roof of the net, Reading now had a 3-1 lead. Nahki Wells walked up next for Huddersfield, knowing that a miss would all but lose his side the match. Curving his penalty with pace into the right hand corner so hard Al-Habsi didn't even move, it was one of the best strikes of the bunch, and kept his team alive.

Liam Moore was next for Reading, and he looked confident as he placed the ball down and lined himself up. Skipping toward the ball during his approach, he leant back at the point of contact and got completely underneath the ball, launching it high, high over the bar, inviting Huddersfield back into the competition. Hope suddenly returned to the Town end, with people suddenly starting to watch the kicks again, and uncover their eyes. Dean Hoyle, sat up high in the stands, closed his eyes and put his hands over his face - it would could down to Aaron Mooy to level up the score. Going with power off the instep, he slammed it into the bottom left corner, sending the keeper the wrong way.

We were back to square one.

Jordan Obita, a left footer, made his way up to put Reading back in the lead. Standing with his hands on his hips at the edge of the penalty area before his kick, Ward was back to hopping around and smacking things inside the goal in front of him. Taking the first half of his run up slow, before adding some pace a few steps before the end, Obita looked to power the ball along the ground in to the bottom right hand corner, but Danny Ward had other ideas, getting down smartly to his left to deny the Reading winger, putting the ball back firmly in Huddersfield's court, who were now just one penalty away from being promoted, and becoming a Premier League team for the first time in their history.

The responsibility would fall to Christopher Schindler.

Asking what compelled him to volunteer to take that kick after he didn't step up at Hillsborough as part of the first five, he said his decision was more down to energy and comfort, than anything else. "You know, against Sheffield, it was such a tough game, and I was so tired, that I didn't feel like taking one of the first five," he said.

"We had 10 days in between to recover and train before the final though, so I was fresh again, and felt solid during the game. When it came to penalties, I felt great, I wasn't tired or hurt. Straight after the whistle I went to the manager and said that I'm going to take one, and he told me it was only the last one remaining. I said yeah, well, I'm going to take it. He asked me if I was sure and I was like well, I was until two seconds ago!" He smiles at me and laughs at this point, to let me know he's joking, before continuing: "It's a decision you make. You have to take this opportunity."

A lot is made of the psychology of walking alone from the halfway line to the penalty box, and how players can get so far in their own heads at this point they psyche themselves out of taking a solid penalty. That wasn't the case for Schindler, but he was talking to himself all the way.

"I was just telling myself to score. Please score. It's an almost perfect scenario, you walk with the possibility to get your fairytale happy ending, and I just felt like, I need to score. I felt pressure too, of course." That last line feels like it's been inserted because Schindler has heard pressure is something normal people feel. In truth, he never even looked mildly panicked throughout his entire walk to the ball, and placed it with minimal fuss, taking his steps back and surveying the scene. While there's thirty thousand people having kittens in front of him, a man worth £350m an emotional wreck in the stands and Captain Jean-Luc Picard of the Starship Enterprise having to put his hand over his mouth out of panic, Schindler didn't look to have so much as a hair out of place. If they ever reboot Bond in German - he's your man.

Settling himself, Schindler took eight steps toward the

ball from his starting position just on the edge of the penalty box, each one marginally faster than the one that preceded it. As he addressed the ball, silence fell momentarily around Wembley.

EPILOGUE:

SMILE A WHILE

"I still have the picture in my mind of the ball hitting the net."

Christopher Schindler is beaming by this point in the story. "I don't remember much after, though. There are so many emotions, the occasion is so big, it's hard to hold all of that in. All the way from the security at the hotel to the size of the stadium and the atmosphere, it's crazy. I'm so thankful to have had that experience."

Passing the ball right into the far left hand corner of the goal, Christopher Schindler scored a penalty that was worth hundreds of millions to his football club, but priceless for all those that support it. Skipping away with his hands in the air, he ripped his shirt off before being mobbed by his team-mates. Danny Ward, a hero in his own right for saving the strike from Obita, was in tears on his knees, crumpled over. There were grown men weeping in the stands, children red in the face and women shrieking with joy. Dean Hoyle, still with his hands covering his face, looked like he'd been 15 rounds with a young Mike Tyson by the time he came up for air. Tears in his eyes, hair out of place - this is what the emotion of football is about. It's not handshakes and slaps on the backs, it's panic attacks and crying. There are no other ways to accurately display that level of collective disbelief.

There was a story that Dean Hoyle told frequently about the first time he saw Schindler after being promoted. He asked him why he decided to take the decisive kick, and Schindler told him that as his record signing, he owed him that much as a form of repayment. "It's like spotting Elvis isn't it, where did he come from?" Hoyle says of that encounter. "I started bawling my eyes out again, he said to me, I had a duty to repay the money you paid for me and I'm just repaying it. To me, what a man."

Trying to play it down when asked about it, Schindler claims it was said more in jest than seriousness. "I think this is something for the media," he jokes, trying to get out of having to tell the story. "Of course when you get the title of the record signing before the season, there is pressure. What I meant was, by spending that much money, he's shown trust in me, so I wanted to give that back in a way. Obviously, it's also luck that you scored the winning penalty, that you're in this situation. I'm not that player who's always seen the most but one day you have the opportunity to shine and this was my opportunity and I took it - that's why I want to thank the chairman for trusting in me and for spending £1.8 million, because I think there was probably someone else on the market where the transfer would have been easier and cost less but as I said, I didn't mean it to sound too serious."

Like it or not, Christopher Schindler is a man that many people have fond memories of now. "That relief when Schindler scored the penalty," Tommy Smith says, looking at the ceiling as he speaks, "I just went to my knees, the relief and the ecstasy all rolled into one, overshadowed that I'd injured my foot. It made me think back to the previous five years of all the stuff that's changed in the club, it was a flashback of what's gone on over the last 5-6 years to where we got to now. It was a very special day, and an even better feeling."

"Do you know something, I can't really describe it properly, but my emotional well-being was screwed." Dean Hoyle is thinking back on that period around Wembley, and how the magnitude of the occasion affected him. "On the morning of Wembley, I woke up in the hotel in London and I'm on Twitter, watching all the Huddersfield fans setting off, and tears are rolling down my face, for no reason, just rolling down my face. I'm thinking, what on earth are you doing?

"It was the level of expectation. We're not talking 10,000, we're talking 30,000 people going to watch Huddersfield. Flying in from all over the world, and it's that level of expectation. You're thinking, shit, this is huge. I also knew we'd got a realistic chance of doing it. When Schindler actually put the ball down to take that penalty, I just thought, if this ball goes in the net, if he nails this, we're in the Premier League - I never ever believed we'd ever do it, but he nailed it. It's like, I can't believe it. The most surreal, out of body experience you can ever imagine because it wasn't expected. It was just one of those surreal moments. It's hard to describe. I've never seen so many adults in tears before in my life. I think they're similar to me, can't believe it.

"Don't be mistaken, either. It was our only opportunity. Fans would have said to me, Dean we'll go again next year. It were never going to happen. It all came together so well. It was a bit of a perfect storm. It was quite fortunate because we did the cheap ticket offer with heavy metal football and it just came together. Electric atmosphere, great home record, got promoted. You might say it was a moment in time, it just all came together. I really needed a coach here who could outperform the players he has at his disposal because most managers are only as good as the players they have on the pitch. Here, our manager exceeds the players on our pitch. They're more than the sum of their parts, and that's what we needed. We got promoted because our lads came together to become the best team in that division. Individually, we didn't have the best players - but we had the best team.

"At the end of the day," Dean continues, "it made me realise how lucky I've been, to be fair, because I have been incredibly fortunate. Football is about fine margins, and if that penalty had gone the wrong side of the post, we would not be sat here today, and it's literally 6 inches that's the difference. That's it. That's football. If the penalty would have gone left hand side of that post, we wouldn't have been here today having this conversation, and that's the fine margins of football. That's the difference, for me, I'm realistic enough to know how we got here. I always think, if you work hard, you've half a chance. It's hard work, there's been some tough times - football is 80% shit, 20% good, and these times do not come around very often. This is probably 1% of the 100%, this is stellar. It's really good. But there's a width of a post in it. It's as simple as that."

What, then, was the alternative? What if Christopher Schindler HAD missed? What if Reading were celebrating while Huddersfield were left broken on the field? It definitely felt like something that Dean had considered to himself.

"The alternative is we probably would have been seriously looking for new owners, because I would have at that point thought I'd have taken the club as far as I could. I knew it was a perfect storm and for us to compete and get into the top flight, you've got to spend a lot more money than we did, so we really had no right to do it. It was David Wagner who said that first, we had no right, and he's not wrong. If we hadn't have got promoted then I'm sure half our squad would have been sold because firstly, the manager would have gone, and you can't blame him, can you? Secondly, a lot of our players have excelled and some would have gone to big paying Championship clubs we can't compete with. Some would have gone to the Premier League, and others maybe back to Germany for big money. That's why when we got promoted, it was so important that penalty went in - it changed this club forever in a short period."

And what about his ownership? Now that Huddersfield Town are a Premier League club, has there been any interest from outside investors?

"There's always people sniffing, but that's what the game is, these days. I've always said all along, if anybody can do it better than me and they've got deeper pockets then look, my job title is the custodian of fans' dreams. If somebody can deliver that better than me, I'd never stand in their way. It'd be the saddest day of my life, but I'm sure especially after promotion, I'm sure whatever happens now, I can look back with fondness with what I've achieved."

Central to this success is the strong working relationship between Dean Hoyle and David Wagner, but even that was a learning curve for the German coach, who's used to a footballing system where one man isn't allowed to own an entire club. "It's strange, it's different, it is, absolutely," David said, when asked about adjusting to that structure. "On one side, you only have to speak with one person, which makes it much more easier, because you can make quick decisions, and on the other side, it's very different to Germany where a lot of board meetings sometimes happen and everyone likes to say something, everyone likes to have a bit of spotlight in Germany, everyone likes to be in the media as well. Sometimes, this causes you more problems and confusion rather than being a help. I worked in both environments and I can say I can handle both, so I think altogether we can be very happy with the channel we have here. It's been a good relationship from the start."

This, of course, can be illustrated best in Hoyle's repeat re-signing of David to bigger and better contracts whenever the club have deemed it necessary.

"This is a credit to Dean that he always wants to show that he's happy with the work we've done so far, and on the other side, he was always aware about what's going on behind the scenes, with other clubs making offers. In the end, I think it paid off for all of us - we are now a Premier League club with a Premier League chairman and manager and back room staff and supporters and players as well. After the season was over and got promoted, it was a very easy decision to stay. It was one meeting with Dean and then it was very clear what it was I wanted to do. We do need to stay honest with ourselves, though, we are all together on one side still the same Championship sized club. We're the football club who are in the Premier League and we will make further steps, but I think we should be very honest with ourselves that there's a lot of work to do and we are playing here with the really big names and usually, we have no right to be here! But we're there and we're ambitious enough to try and do our best to stay there."

What, then, stands out for Wagner most about last season? "We had our setbacks over the season," he says, "as well as in the period before we got this final win against Wolves, where we qualified for the play-offs. We lost the last two games without a goal, 2-0 against Birmingham and then 3-0 at home against Cardiff. There was also the red card to Danny Ward, so that was a setback for the first leg. We had our setback in the second leg, when we were 1-0 down against Sheffield after the header. We had even our setback in the final when we missed Hef's penalty and they were 3-1 up, so what makes the story even bigger, and what I loved most about the season, is that apart from the low budget, apart from the inexperience this group had, apart from the group being very young that achieved this success, the group was always able to bounce back after setbacks. This makes the story even bigger for myself and has shown the character of this group, never give up attitude and fighting spirit to try it until the last second, and this was extraordinary for sure."

"It's changed massively," Tommy Smith says of the club. "I think I've been here the longest in the team, six years, give or take. I've seen quite a lot of changes. When I first arrived, I was training on an old cow field, so I've seen it develop over the years. It's a fantastic club from where it was to what it is now, the change has been great. I've seen a lot of players come in and a lot of players go out, and obviously when the manager turns up it was the biggest change of them all. I have to say what he's done to the club has been nothing short of amazing. Transformed it from top to bottom and everything, the food aspect, the training times, it's been well documented what he's done to this club. He's certainly changed it for the better. He took a team who were tipped for relegation last season and coached us to the Premier League - I don't think I can say much more about the influence he's had than that.

"I'm most proud of the bunch of people I've had the journey with," he continues, when asked what his abiding memory from last season might be. "The team, the staff, I don't just mean the team who go on the pitch on Saturday and play, some people may argue the team who play have got us promoted but it's certainly not the case, there's a lot bigger picture that got us to that level last season. The people we work with day in day out, the video team, the medical team, the food team, it takes a team effort to get to places where we are. There's a lot of sides who've fell sort over the years who've had the budgets no one else has had, and had the players no one else has had, but it doesn't just happen on the pitch on the Saturday with 11 players, it stems back much further than that. It's important we recognise everybody who made promotion a possibility, and I'm completely proud and honoured to be captain of such a special bunch. I'm completely proud of everything that I've achieved and the club's achieved as a whole. When I first joined the club it was a case of staying in division, so I've seen it all. It's been a phenomenal journey for myself and one I can look back on with immense pride. I certainly don't feel as though the journey has ended now we're in the Premier League, either - I want to push on as much as I can with this club."

A proud period for the long-term staff of the club, too, they've seen and lived it all as much as the players have. Before completing the interview process with them, I asked what stands out most from last season? How have their jobs been changed? What story will they first tell their grandchildren about the season they were part of Huddersfield Town's run to the Premier League, and what that meant to them at the time?

"I don't think I can look past the play-offs, to be honest, as obvious as that is," David Threlfall-Sykes tells me. "I'm in a really fortunate position because due to all the broadcasting commitments that need to be fulfilled immediately after those type of high-profile televised fixtures, I'm usually brought down to pitch side before the end of the game. When we were at Hillsborough, I got to stand just behind our group in a line, so going through that shootout with them was an experience I'll never forget. The scenes at the end of that game were amazing.

"Since promotion it's been really interesting, because it's as new to us as it is to all the players and everything. The figures have shot up in my department, for example. Our audience reach has absolutely gone through the roof. We're about 70% up. Bear in mind that last year was a high figure for us because we were doing so well, the figure has gone up by about 70% across the board, whether it's social, whether it's web platforms, email shots. Roughly 70%. The demographic's changed too, that's the big thing for us. We've gone from around 95% UK audience, 92-95% last year to last month's figures were 69% so there's a big, big leap in people abroad who are now interested in Huddersfield Town.

"America is a big area for us, because nominally we have an American manager and we have an American midfielder now. It's fantastic for us. China obviously have provided our new main sponsor, so that's a completely new market for us. It'd be absolutely remiss to say that we know completely what we're doing over there because obviously China's a very different country to ours, but we're learning. That's what this whole experience has been about to me - learning.

"Equally, I remember being in the tunnel at Wembley when Hefele had his penalty saved, and I can't quite put my finger on why, but I had this level of confidence in the players that I've never had before for another collection of Town players. They're all really great characters and they're brilliant footballers, but penalties are a bit mad, aren't they? Regardless, there was something about that group that gave me this weird level of confidence. I remember thinking to myself that it was all going to be alright because Danny Ward will definitely stop one. I was absolutely sure of it. I had such faith in him as an individual at that moment in time, I'm just glad it worked out the way it did. Those emotions and thoughts won't ever leave me."

Similarly, for Sue Beaumont, it's less about what happened and more about what's happening now - the changes and the growth. Her job has completely changed, just as the club has. "I've been a fan for over fifty years so it's something I was hoping might happen. I was fortunate enough to see us play the last time we were in the top flight, and I remember watching the likes of George Best, which was incredible. When you think that going forward, people here now will be watching the George Best of today, Harry Kane or someone, it's quite something. It's come full circle and back again. We were a long time in the doldrums, so credit to the investment and the choices and decisions that have been made, we've got something really special going. Hopefully we can stay up and make it count, go again next year. The work should take care of itself a bit better if we do, because we've got everything up and running for this level now."

Usually after a match, Andy Brook has to drive the van back - but after Wembley, he got somebody to cover for him. "After the penalties I was straight on the pitch, celebrating with everyone. I managed to get one of the bus drivers to drive the van back so I could get on the coach with everybody else, and that was my highlight really. We were sat on the bus for four hours, we were all drinking a few beers and singing songs. It was really good, enjoying that together knowing how hard the season had been. They're the days you don't want to miss really. This was special, we got to the Premier League, which to be fair, nobody really believed it after, did they? I didn't believe it after. It was only David Wagner could have done it. I don't think anyone else could have done what he did. I don't think it'll happen again. I think for teams like Huddersfield on a small budget ... I don't think it'll happen again, I really don't. I think the togetherness and everything else got through it."

At the celebration parade in Huddersfield town centre at St George's Square, there was a moment where David Wagner singled Brooky out, who was backstage with his family. Held the day after the play-off final in conjunction with an open-top bus parade through the town, West Yorkshire police estimated that 25,000 people turned out to welcome the team home, and celebrate their new elite status. Just as the town has forever done, it was once again punching above its weight, and it wasn't scared to shout about it.

With the players on the stage with the trophy, the manager wanted the crowd to chant for the kitman, who only begrudgingly made his way to the front. "I think he knows I don't like that sort of thing," Brooky says, still sounding a little uncomfortable about it all. "I was standing behind the stage with my two little ones, 4 and 2, I think one of them needed the toilet. I'm trying to find the toilet and I hear him saying, 'This guy's been in the club a long time,' and I'm thinking, please, please don't be me. He made me go up regardless. It's not me, I don't like all that. I just like to be in the background and out of the way, but it's nice to be recognised at the same time.

It just shows you what a special man he is."

With less time than the rest to adjust for a season in the Premier League, it's been a whirlwind last six months for Huddersfield Town, who've had to change and grow to take their place in the biggest sports league in the world. Having recruited well in the summer and given David Wagner the tools he desired to tackle their latest obstacle, the club were again written off and patronised by the pundits on television, the radio and online, who all but relegated the club before a ball had even been kicked. You would think, given how Huddersfield reacted the last time that happened, that folk would learn not to make the same mistake twice – but it's not going to be something bothering anyone at the club too much. They've kept their core together, and they know what they're capable of when they work together better than anybody else. Underestimate them at your peril – we know at least that much to remain true.

"We like to lead at this club," says Dean Hoyle, "not follow. I think the way we've done it is different and now finally people are trying to follow our example, but it's not quite as easy as that. It's like, kicking against the establishment, isn't it? Doing it a different way. That turns me on." Not shying away from going toe-to-toe with the sheikhs and the oligarchs in the Premier League, there's a fire in Hoyle's eye that was likely present when he set Clintons in his sights – there's no prizes for guessing how that one turned out.

It's hard to sum up such a season, with the highs and lows, the doubts and the obstacles, but there's one thing David Wagner said that may put a full stop on the story best – and it's only fitting that he should have the final word:

"At the end this is what everyone likes, this attitude. We as a football club have shown that this is where we stand, and what it's all about. This should be part of our identity, and part of what we stand for. It's bigger than just football, for definite, because it includes the people of our town. This is what we will have to confirm not only in this season to come, but for the next years in this football club - to really give yourself an identity of what the Terrier is all about. People might not have known what that meant before, but they do now, and not just in Huddersfield or England, but across the world. We have made people take notice of what the Terrier Spirit is, and what we're all about. Huddersfield Town can be proud again."

ACKNOWLEDGEMENTS

While it may be my name on the front of the book, in truth, this piece of work has been a complete and utter collaboration from start to finish, and it would be remiss of me not to take the time to thank those who helped make this possible.

Firstly, as is only right and correct, I'm forever in debt to my mother, to whom this book is of course dedicated. Without her drive and unflinching desire to see her son reach his potential, there is not a single chance I'd ever have had the capacity to ever complete a project of this size. Never the type of person to expect anything less than the highest standard - as that is what she demands of herself - my work rate, attitude and willingness to push my own boundaries can solely be contributed to her. For that, not only am I better off, but forever thankful. I can only hope that I can do enough to make her proud in return.

My entire career is built on the back of a life-long passion and love for football, and without the influence of my father, those feelings may never have fully developed. The love for this game that we share bonds us in a way that is unbreakable, and there is nobody else on the planet with whom I'd rather experience the sport. It's quite something to be that infatuated with something that you choose to dedicate your life to analysing and documenting it, but that goes some way to explaining just how special that aspect of my relationship with my old man is, and just how much it means to me.

To my baby sister - who has, to be completely honest, contributed to this project in absolutely no tangible way whatsoever - your company, encouragement and unconditional love has been a more than welcome distraction throughout. You never fail to put a smile on my face and lift my mood even when it is at its very worst. Those that know me best will know how difficult a task that can be. I don't know what I ever did to deserve a sibling who is as pure and full of good as you are, but it's never something I take for granted. There is no doubt in my mind that you'll go on to be better and more successful than us all - I can't wait to watch that happen.

There has been nobody who's looked forward to this book being released more than my grandfather, who is the finest man I'll ever know. His support, enthusiasm and pride are all you could ever wish for, and making him happy remains one of my proudest achievements. He continues to be the person I hero worship the most, and if I'm able to amount to even half of what he does, I'll have done extremely well. I must also thank my grandmother, who even in absence remains my moral compass, and a reminder that goodness shall forever be rewarded. I owe so much to you both.

My aunties, Sharan and Manreesh, are walking proof that intelligence, success and good personality aren't mutually exclusive, and my life is far richer for having you both in it to take inspiration from. I am not an easy man to push, and aren't often one to come out of my shell, but you've always managed to prize that from me with little to no effort. You have both had an invaluable influence on my life, providing guidance when I've needed it most, and there are few people I enjoy being myself around more than you two. Thank you for always allowing me that.

Having grown up in Leeds, the majority of my close

friends support an alternative side from West Yorkshire, but have remained supportive of this project throughout, despite themselves. Even when Huddersfield were doing well at the expense of their side, you showed a level of maturity that wasn't anticipated. Without knowing it, your friendship and companionship - whether that involves having the piss taken out of me or not - is not taken for granted. Lucas, Ryan, Creasy, Adam and Ben - thanks for everything, and I hope you're still enjoying the Championship.

In truth, my time following Huddersfield on a regular basis only came about when, largely on a whim, my friend James - a real Town fan, unlike myself - suggested we get season tickets a few years back, long before either of us knew David Wagner even existed. Since then, it has been quite the journey. We've celebrated each and every goal with a giant hug, shared precarious journeys to and from away grounds across the country, and took a trip to Wembley that I'm sure neither of us will ever forget. Cheers lad, I hope this book has done your team justice - thanks for allowing me along for the ride. I would promise to try and stop making us late on a match day but, we both know that isn't going to happen.

David Burrill and Roger Arnold of Great Northern Books, this would never have seen the light of day without your input. I'm sure Roger thought I was somewhat misguided when I called across with an idea for a book about Huddersfield Town being promoted to the Premier League a week into March, but here we are. As a first time author, this has been some learning curve for me, and I'm not one shy of asking a question, so I can only thank David for his impeccable patience throughout. You have both made this experience far more pleasurable than it may have been otherwise, and it has been a total joy working with you. My editor, Ross Jamieson – thank you for going the extra mile to make sure all the right words were in the right order. John Early, who provided our photography - your work is of an unbelievable quality. Your images are the perfect visual representation of this story, and the book would be a much less enjoyable object without the inclusion of those shots. Thank you for agreeing to work with us.

To the people at Huddersfield Town, who never once got annoyed when I called asking questions, and did all they could during what is probably the busiest period in the club's modern history to accommodate my every request - thank you for allowing me to tell your story. As a son of this town, it has been an immense privilege, and an experience I will forever hold dear. Luke Cowan, David Threlfall-Sykes, Sean Jarvis, Sue Beaumont and Andy Brook, your cooperation has been invaluable, and won't be forgotten. Dean Hoyle, thank you for agreeing to provide the foreword for this project, and most of all, not walking out of our meeting upon hearing I was a Tottenham fan. Working in football, and peeping behind the curtain of this game, there are questionable characters at every turn - you are an example to all of them, and a credit to both the football team and the town. David Wagner, your openness and honesty is a breath of fresh air, and there are precious few people I enjoy speaking to about the game more. There is no doubt in my mind that you will go on to have a long and successful career in the game, wherever that may take you in the future - as long as it isn't Arsenal, you'll always have a fan in me. Also, I forgive you for laughing in my face during the summer of 2016 when I suggested you might have one eye on the top six - after that interview, I went straight to the bookies.

Lastly, to fans of Huddersfield and the people of this town, thank you for pre-ordering and buying this book. It genuinely astounds me that anybody would ever be interested in anything that I may have to say. My only intention in doing this was to do your club and our town the justice they deserve in light of their achievement - hopefully this book has delivered on that.

TERRIER FANS

Ken Abbott

Arron Afsar

Stephanie Airs

Richard Ambler

Cambi Anderson

John Andrews

Simon Andrews

Neil Archer

Stuart Ardrey

Andrew Armitage

John, Thomas & Joe Ashley

Alan Ashton

Stuart Asquith

Cole Augustine

Mr Gurdip Singh Bains

Dr Manreesh Bains

Mrs Mohinder Kaur Bains

Ms Sharan Bains

Navdeep Bains

Michael Balmforth

Howard Bamforth

William Bamforth

Elliot "Beautiful Face Guy" Barker

Michael Barker

Stacey Barker

Stephen Barker

Keith Barlow

Frank Barr

Paul Barrett

Edward Battye

Herbie Battye

Wilfred "Pip" Battye

Harry Beaumont

Peter Beaumont

Robin Beaumont

Stan Beben

Craig Beetham

Michael Betony

Clive Blakey

Simon Blakey

David Blamires

David Boardall

Anthony & Edward Booth - The Horbury Terriers

Elly Booth

David Boothroyd

Helen Bottomley

Emma Bownas

Martin Bowness

Chris Boylan

Chris Bradley

Paul Bradley

Rod Bradley

Martin Breslin

David & Rhona Broadhead

Eddie Broadley

David Brook

Chris Bruce

Hugh Burton

Paul Butcher

David Edward Byrne

Robert Cartwright

Gerald Cawthra

Dave Chambers

Lewis Christian

Frankie, Claire and Abigail Clark

Roger Clark

Charlie Clayton

Amy Mikaela Clegg

David and Mavis Clegg

Ben Coates

Graham Coates

Tom Cocking

Graham Coldwell

Peter & Sarah Collinson

Tim Coop

Edward and William Cran

Mark Croft

Harold Crossley

John David Crossley

Kieran Crowfoot

Andrew Daisey

John G Davies

Malcolm Dawes

Peter & Paul Dawson

Philip Denton

William & Thomas Donaghy

Alan Doyle

John Drew

Clark Eastwood

Lottie Anais Eastwood

Adam Luke Ellis

Don Farmer

Andrew N. Fawbert

Joshua Fenn

Richard Fenn

Graham Ferguson

Robert Finnigan

Robert Firth

Danny Fisher

Oliver Fisher

Shaun Fisher

Garry Flanagan

Sean Flanagan

Andrew Foster

James Andrew Foster

Neil Frederick Foster

Callum Fox

Dennis Frear

Luke Gallagher

Marcus Garside

Tony Garside

Brian Garton

Victor Gembala

Ibrahim George

Karl George

Stephen George

Billy Gerrard

Paul Gerrard

Jonathan Gillespie

Paul Gillespie

John D. Glew

Ian. M. Gould

Jonathan Gould

Nigel Gould

Richard Green

Daniel Grimes

Michael Grove

Richard Grove

Jeffrey Gunson

Andrew Haigh

Matthew Haigh

Granville Hall

Lauren Kate Hall

Phil Hall

Richard Hall

David Hampshire

Henry Hanson

Trevor Hardcastle

Brian, Alison & Jill Hargreaves

Ross Hargreaves

David and George Hebblethwaite

John, Claire and Ian Hebblethwaite

Brian Hebblethwaite (in memory of)

Michael Hegarty

Paul Hegarty

Joshua Harry Hellawell

AJ Hemingway

Lydia Hemingway

Edward Hennell

Christopher Hepworth

Lewis Hepworth

Matthew Hepworth

Peter Hepworth

Beverley Hey

Derek Hey

John Higginbottom

Andrew Hirst

Chris Hirst

Daniel Hirst

Greg Hirst

Michael Hirst

Stephen Hirst

James Hobson

Marjorie Hobson

Shaun Benjamin Hodgson

Clive Holt

George Holt

Lee Holt

Norman Hopwood

Richard Hopwood

Ian Howcroft

William Howcroft

John Howell

Alan Hudders

Chris Huffer

Christopher Huffer

David John Huggins

William Hurst

Dominic Jacques

Geoffrey Johnson

Graham Johnson

Liam Jones

Paul Jones

Andy and George Kaye

Roger Kaye

John Keen

Helen Kelly

Nigel Kenworthy

Thomas Kenworthy

Brian Kilner (in memory of)

Andrew Kirk

Thomas Kirk

Phil Kitchingman

Peter Laidlaw

Graham Large

Robert Large

Trish Laverty

Tony Lee

John Lewis

Graham Lister

John Terry Little

George Thomas Lockwood

James Lockwood

Stephen Lockwood

David Longbottom

Urban Lundquist

Gez Lunn

Brian Owen Macer

Leo Maciver

Peter Mackle

Christopher Maguire

Billy Mallinson

David Marsh

John Marsh

Bill Marshall

John Mason

Richard Mason

Colin McCabe

Brian McCarthy

Alex McFarlane

Brian and Noreen McGuin

Kevin McMahon

Roger Mead

Robert Mellor

Andy Menzies

D,T & J Merriman

John Metcalfe

Michael & Anne Miller

Paul Moon

David Moorhouse

Freddy Abraham Mordecai

Steve Morris

Richard Barry Mortimer

Dave Mortram

Tom Naylor

Lee Nestor

Myles Neville

Andrew Nichols

Robert Nichols 1951-2016

D F Noble

J R Noble

David North

Patrick O'Reilly

Brian Oram

Allan Osbourne

Ian Parkin

Roger Pashby

Raymond Peace

Richard Peace

Wayne Graham Peacock

Hilary Pearson

Nick Pedley

Edward Alfie Peel

Robert Pepper

Jack Antony Pickford

James Pickles

Archie Pierson

Glynn Pinchbeck

Mark C Pogson

Steve Pogson

Patricia Pollard

Peter Pollard

Anthony Preece

George Preece

Matthew Preece

SarahJane Preece

Sophie Preece

Eric Preston

Ray Pullen

John Randall

Melvyn Rawnsley

Peter John Ray

Lee Redman

Alex Rhodes

David Rhodes

David Roberts

James (Robbo) Roberts

Noel Roberts

Dan Robinson

Glen Robinson

James Robinson

Charlotte Rogers

Dodge and Tony Rogers

Franky Rogers

Izaak Rout

Simon Rout

Keith Rowbottom

Sasha Rowbottom

Jason Rowlands

James Ruscoe

John Rushworth

Kevin Rushworth

Mark Rushworth

Peter Rushworth

Carol Sanderson

Neil Antony Scorah

Philip Scott

Jonathan
Selwood-Hogg

Alex Senior

Katy Senior

James Sharland

Chris & Rach Sharp

Dale Shaw

David Shaw

Robert Shaw

Samantha Shaw

Stephen Shaw

John Sheard

Trev Shields

David Siddall

Finola Siddall

James Simpson

Tony and Marc Sinfield

Paul Skilbeck

Kieran Smith

Rob Smith

Oliver Spencer

Garry M Spivey

Paul Stead

Richard Stead

Rob Stead (Oscarbravo)

Richard Colin Stocks

Steven Suddick

Richard'Dickie' Sutton

Suva House Queens
Square

Andrew Roberts
Swailes

Alister Sykes

Geoff Sykes

Glyn Sykes

Chris Tarmu

Stuart Tattersfield

Mark J Taylor

Martin Taylor

Richard Taylor

Robert C Taylor

Andy & Sarah-Jane
Thewlis

Craig Thompson

George Thompson

Martin Thornton

Peter Thornton

Steven Thornton

Anne Tinker

David M Townend

Linzi Townend

Paul M Townend

Stephen Townend

Harold Tulley (Shedds}

Andrew Turton

Daniel Vasey

George Waga

Ian Walker

Nicola Walker

Ben Wallis

Paul Walton

David R Ward

Mrs Bev Ward

Tim Ward

Flt Lt John M Ward RAF
(Retd)

Andrew & Harry Warren

Ciarán Warters

Stuart Washington.

Luke Watson

Michael Watson

Adam Whitehead

Rod Whiteley

Tony Wilby
(In Memory of)

Reverend David Wilding

Nick Wilding

Dominic Wilkinson

Mary Wilkinson

Ava Willans

Maisie Willans

Joshua Williams

Nathan Williams

Neil Wilsher

David Richard Wood

Luca David George
Wood

Peter John Wood

Andrew Woodcock

Helen Woodcock

Nigel Woodcock

Vaughan Woolfitt

James Yates

Phillip Yates

Bloke, Little Bloke and
Whippy

Chris

Frenchy

George

John

Matthew

Miriam & Eileen

Queenie

Smurf69

Steve, Jude and Freddie

TerrierSpirit.com